Research Skills Series

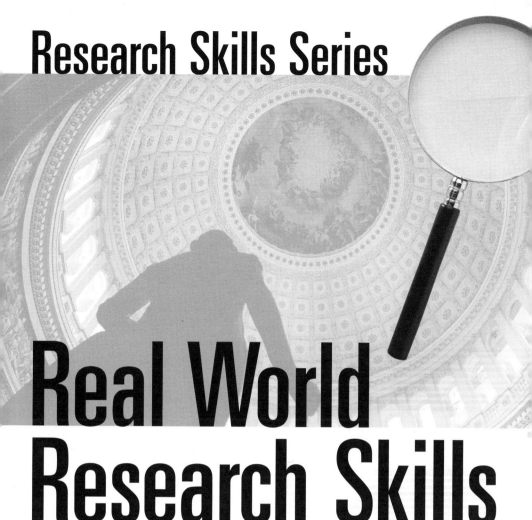

Real World
Research Skills

An Introduction to Factual, International,
Judicial, Legislative, and Regulatory Research

By Peggy Garvin

TheCapitol.Net, Inc. is a non-partisan firm that annually provides continuing professional education and information for thousands of government and business leaders that strengthens representative government and the rule of law.

Our publications and courses, written and taught by current Washington insiders who are all independent subject matter experts, show how Washington works.™ Our products and services can be found on our web site at *<www.TheCapitol.Net>*.

Additional copies of Real World Research Skills can be ordered directly from the publisher. Secure online ordering is available on the web site, *<www.RealWorldResearchSkills.com>*.

Citation Form—URLs: We use a standard style for all web addresses, also known as Uniform Resource Locators (URLs). URLs appear in text next to the first mention of the resource being described, and are surrounded with open and close angle brackets.

For URLs that have the standard web addressing form at the beginning of the URL of "http://www." we show only the initial "www." For example, the URL "http://www. domainname.com" will appear in text and tables as "*<www.domainname.com>*."

For URLs that begin with anything other than "www.," such as "http://thomas.loc.gov," the URL will appear in text and tables as "*<http://thomas.loc.gov>*." For example, the URL "http://www3.domain.gov" will appear in text and tables as "*<http://www3.domain.gov>*."

Design and production by Zaccarine Design, Inc., Evanston, IL; 847-864-3994.

LCCN: 2006923332

Paperback: 1587330075, ISBN 13: 978-1-58733-007-0
Hardcover: 1587330938, ISBN 13: 978-1-58733-093-3

About the Author

Peggy Garvin is an independent information consultant. Her company, Garvin Information Consulting, provides training, writing, and consulting to help professionals make the best use of the wealth of U.S. government information online. Peggy has worked with government information, libraries, and information technology over her twenty-year career with the Library of Congress Congressional Research Service and in the private sector. She earned her Master of Library Science degree from Syracuse University.

Peggy contributes to TheCapitol.Net's *Congressional Deskbook* and edits the annual reference book *United States Government Internet Manual* (Lanham, MD: Bernan Press). Her monthly column, "The Government Domain," appears in the law and technology webzine, LLRX.com.

Contents

Chapter 6 Experts and Insiders 81

Table of Web Sites 89
Index 100

Scope

This book compiles basic advice, techniques, reference information, and resources to help working professionals find accurate information quickly. It is written particularly for those whose work involves tapping into federal government information. The book began as a set of materials for TheCapitol.Net's seminar, "Research Skills for the Real World." It is designed to be used as a complement to that seminar or independently as a desk reference.

The Introduction and first chapter cover practical principles of research and online searching, including the general search engines. These sections include checklists and advice that are applicable to many different research tasks and many different databases and search engines.

The second, third, and fourth chapters present resources for federal legislative, judicial, and executive branch research.

The fifth chapter covers starting points for state and international research on the web.

The final chapter, "Experts and Insiders," has tips for tapping into that vital Washington information resource: people.

In our knowledge economy, more and more people—with a wide range of education and experience—are moving into jobs that require some information-gathering skills. The research training provided at many schools lays a foundation, but often does not prepare us for the varied demands of the working world. This book is not intended to cover academic research resources, nor is it a comprehensive listing of Washington research resources. It supplies advice based on working knowledge and experience, and pointers to good places to start one's search.

We hope it will be useful to you. If you have suggestions for additions or changes to the book, please contact us: Publisher, TheCapitol.Net, PO Box 25706, Alexandria, VA 22313-5706, fax: 202-466-5370, email: deskbook@thecapitol.net

Introducing the
Research Skills Series

We have provided icons to alert you to important points.

Search Guide
gives you answers on the search process.

Research Tips
are practical hints to make your search easier.

Information Resources
are places for you to look for specific answers to your questions.

Checklist
is a quick list of ways to improve your searching.

Reference Information
describes and defines basic information.

Introduction

Before You Start Your Research

A research project, small or large, begins with either an assignment from someone else or with your own recognition that you need more information. Either way, you can make your research more efficient and effective by assessing both the information need and the available information sources before you dive into a search engine or pick up the phone to make that first call.

Assessing the information need:

- Do you understand the question? That may sound painfully obvious but, whether you receive a research assignment from someone else or identify the need yourself, it is important to restate and understand the questions to be answered.
- What is the scope of the question? This is particularly important to pin down if you are doing research for someone else. What do they already know about the topic and what is still to be discovered? Do they need a basic overview or in-depth analysis? Current data or historical trends?
- What format is expected? Do you need one quick statistic or a source for data that can be imported into in your own spreadsheet and updated regularly?

- What type of documentation—of either the answer or the research process used—is expected? (For example, you may need to keep a list of all sources checked or save web pages that could disappear the next day.)
- When is the information needed? If there is a quick deadline, which part of the information need is it most important to fill? Is this an ongoing project, or a one-time need?

Assessing the information sources:

- How do your answers to the above questions dictate what resources you can use?
- Are there information sources that should be tapped first due to timing? (For example, you may need to reach a news reporter before the late afternoon deadline rush, or call an office in a different time zone before they close for the day.)
- What staff and money constraints (in addition to time constraints) will affect your approach?

Chapter 1

Going Beyond Google

General search engines have quickly become the default information resource for many people. But they are not always the best choice and—even when we do use them—we often are not using them optimally or with a full understanding of how they work.

This chapter offers information and guidance on using search engines and on searching in general.

§1.00 Know the Full Range of Information Sources

General search engines—such as Google or Yahoo!—are so easy to use that it can be tempting to try to use them for any research problem, whether appropriate or not. Remember the old saying, "to the man with a hammer, everything looks like a nail"? Efficient research makes use of the best resources for the problem, and the best is not always a general search engine. The full spectrum of research resources includes, but is not limited to:

- Free web resources sponsored by educational, advocacy, government, commercial, and other entities.
- For-fee commercial online services such as CQ.com or LexisNexis.
- "Offline" resources—people and print.

This book describes information resources of all sorts, including general search engines.

§1.01 Major Search Engines

TIP: *Try the advanced search option, if one is available. The menu options on advanced search screens often make it easier for you to construct an effective search.*

Ask.com

<www.ask.com>

Ask.com, formerly called Ask Jeeves, is a basic search engine that also provides features such as news and shopping searches. Search results include suggestions for alternative search words to broaden or narrow your search.

Dogpile

<www.dogpile.com>

Dogpile searches across Ask.com, Google, Yahoo!, and others. It provides an easy way to search multiple search engine databases at once, and to see how different search engines deliver different results.

Google

<www.google.com>

Google is an extremely popular search engine. It is fast, powerful, and has a simple interface. Behind the simple interface, Google is capable of complex searching. See the Advanced Search options screen. A site called

§1.02 Limitations of General Search Engines

General search engines help researchers find the web addresses, or URLs, needed to retrieve specific web sites. General search engines serve as indexes to a lot of the popular information available via the web. But searchers should be aware of their limitations:

- **Search engines cover only a fraction of the content on the web.** If a search engine does not find information you need, you can't conclude that the information is not on the web. The web is simply too large and dynamic for any search engine to index it comprehensively. Some information, such as that on sites requiring user-registration or behind a corporate firewall, is off-limits to search engines.

- **Search engines do not necessarily have the most current information.** Because it takes time to find and index information on the web, search engines do not provide the most recent news or changes to web content.

- **There is no quality filter for the information on the web.** Content of any kind—factual, scholarly, satirical, deceptive— resides on the web. Much of it has no label or clear indicator of purpose, target audience, or author credentials. Sifting through and evaluating the varied content delivered by general search engines consumes valuable time.

- **Search results are subject to manipulation both by the search engine and by those who post content to the web.** Because searches often result in hundreds or thousands of results, the results near the top are the ones that most people consult. Due to the open nature of the web, anyone from marketers to pranksters may affect what gets ranked near the top.

Soople (*<www.soople.com>*)—which is not affiliated with Google—makes it even easier to take advantage of these advanced search options.

MSN Search

<http://search.msn.com>

MSN Search includes options to search just the web, just the news, or just Microsoft's encyclopedia, *Encarta.* Most of the options for advanced searching, such as limiting the search results to a particular language, are under the "Search Builder" menu. MSN Search also offers an easy route to

§1.03 Handy Guides

InfoPeople Search Engine Guides:
- **Best Search Tools Chart**
  <http://infopeople.org/search/chart.html>
- **Best Search Engines Quick Guide**
  <http://infopeople.org/search/guide.html>

These concise guides to search engine features can be used interactively in web format or can be printed out in PDF format. (InfoPeople is a project of the state of California to make the Internet more accessible to citizens through libraries.)

using its Spanish-language interface and to limiting results to Spanish-language only.

Yahoo! Search

<http://search.yahoo.com>

Yahoo! Search is probably the closest rival to Google. Like Google, it offers an advanced search and special features such as a search for images on the web.

§1.10 Know How to Start from Scratch

Researching in a subject area that is new to you can be particularly challenging. You may lack the expertise needed to evaluate general search engine results, and you may not know where else to begin. The following web sites can be effective finding aids (resources that help you find the sources you need to do your work).

Several of these resources are provided by academic libraries. Library web sites often provide selective lists of books, databases, and web sites in areas of interest to students and faculty. Access to some links may be limited to the campus users; this is usually indicated with a note or symbol.

§1.11 Starting Points on the Web

General Subject Guides:
- Librarian's Index to the Internet, *<http://lii.org>*. This extensive directory of links to selected web sites is funded by a federal grant, the California and Washington state libraries, and others.

- The Internet Public Library (IPL), *<www.ipl.org>*, is a directory of selected web sites on topics such as business, education, health, and government. IPL also has research guides and a directory of links to newspapers and magazines online. The site is sponsored by the University of Michigan School of Information.

Public Policy and Government:

- Public Agenda Issue Guides, *<www.publicagenda.org/issues/ issuehome.cfm>*. Developed by the nonpartisan organization Public Agenda, these guides include a "sources and resources" section for further research on topics such as education, health care, and campaign finance.
- Stateline.org Issues, *<www.stateline.org>*. The Issues section of this site has current news and "useful links" on policy topics of interest to the states, such as crime, energy, and transportation.
- University of Michigan Documents Center, *<www.lib.umich.edu/ govdocs/index.html>*. This library site is an extensive guide to information resources on federal, state, and international government topics.

Law:

- FindLaw, *<www.findlaw.com>*. This free web site from the Thomson publishing company provides background information and resource guides for legal topics, with sections tailored to the public and legal professionals.
- Georgetown University Law "Find It Fast" Page, *<www.ll. georgetown.edu/find/>*. The Georgetown Law Library's guides to books, databases, and web sites cover a wide variety of legal topics.

§1.12 Starting Points in Print

- *United States Government Internet Manual* (Lanham, MD: Bernan Press). Extensive guide to federal government web sites. Updated annually. See *<www.bernanpress.com>*.
- *Washington Information Directory* (Washington: CQ Press). A guide to Washington contacts from federal agencies, Congress, and private interest groups. Updated annually; also available online for a fee. See *<www.cqpress.com>*.

§1.20 **Know What You Are Searching**

§ 1.30 covers *how* to search. But, before you begin searching, it is important to understand *what* you are searching. You wouldn't look in a woodworkers' tool catalog for a good deal on the latest MP3 player, would you? Of course not. An inappropriate choice of a web database is not always so obvious.

Some examples:

- Google Uncle Sam <*www.google.com/unclesam*>, with its "stars and stripes" logo, is a popular search engine for finding federal government information. However, it only includes federal sites that end in .gov or .mil, and there are federal web sites—such as those of the National Defense University and the USDA Forest Service—that do not use .gov or .mil. Google Uncle Sam also searches state and local government web sites that end in .gov.

- As discussed in § 2.43, many of the congressional appropriations "earmarks" (special spending instructions for specific projects or recipients) are not in the text of the appropriations bills. Searching a database of congressional bills will not help you find an earmark. Instead, you need to search a database that includes the appropriations conference manager's statement.

§1.21 **How Do You Learn about a Database's Content?**

- ✔ Read all available information the database provides, such as any "help" or "about" pages on the web site.

- ✔ Conduct test searches to plumb the depths of the database. For example, if a person or company is not listed in a database, try searching on the name of a similar person or company or the name of a very famous person or company. Test searches such as these can help you discover limitations in a database's coverage.

- ✔ Call the sponsor of the database or others skilled in using the data.

- ✔ Take training classes offered for the databases you will need to use often.

§1.31 What Do You Need to Know Before You Search?

Some of the questions you will want to have answered are:

✔ How do I search on a phrase, such as "red cross"?

✔ Does the search engine find word variations—such as "vote," "voter," and "voting"—or do I need to search on each of these variations?

✔ Are there any special searches—such as searching on numbers or legal citations—that are handled differently?

§1.30 Know How to Search the Database

Many web sites offer the same blank search box, but the way each processes your search words can be different.

Type the phrase **red cross** into Google, and your top results will include the phrase **red cross**, with the words next to each other and in that order—American Red Cross, International Committee of the Red Cross, British Red Cross, etc.

Type the same phrase into the *Congressional Record* on GPO Access, <*www.gpoaccess.gov*>, and your search may find a statement about "National Wear Red Day" that uses the word **red** many times but never uses the word cross.

Why? On GPO Access, you must type a phrase in quotes to ensure that your results include that exact phrase. If you type just those two words in Google, the search engine assumes that results with the exact phrase are most relevant and puts them at the top. Google also assumes that both words must be in the most relevant search results.

§1.32 Help!

To learn how to use the database, read the help. This is what the experts do. Examples of search engine help:

• Google Help Center <*www.google.com/help/index.html*>

• Yahoo! Help <*http://help.yahoo.com/help/us/ysearch/*>

§1.33 Planning and Conducting an Online Search

✔ **Envision the answer.** What would the answer to your question look like? Will it be technical or popular literature, or a set of numerical data? Who would write or speak about your topic? An advocacy group, a political scientist, an industry specialist, a local journalist, or a congressional committee? Thinking broadly about these questions will help you choose a source to search and to come up with effective words for your search.

✔ **Use more than one search engine or online database.** Unless you have a very narrow question, such as, "who is the Comptroller General of the United States," you will often benefit from searching more than one source. This is particularly true when using general search engines, because no single search engine covers the entire web and each indexes some material that the others do not.

✔ **Learn from the results of your first search.** Searching is an iterative process. Review your initial search results and see if there are words you should add or drop.

✔ **Try variations on your first search.** Even slight variations will almost always produce different results in a general search engine or large database.

✔ **Think of common synonyms or alternate terms.** For example, the concept *global warming* might also be expressed as *global change, climate change*, or *greenhouse effect*.

✔ **Eliminate ambiguity in your search.** *Turkey* may be a country or a bird. *China* may be a country or a porcelain material. If you cannot come up with a less ambiguous alternate word, try adding other words to limit to the sense of the word that you intend; for example, *turkey dinner* or *turkey hunting*. Another option is to choose an online source that is limited in subject coverage. For example, a search on *turkey* in the State Department web site will find background and policy news on the country of Turkey, with only a few irrelevant results involving the annual White House pardoning of a Thanksgiving turkey. A third option is to use advanced search techniques to exclude results with the sense you do not intend, such as excluding any results with the word *Thanksgiving*.

§1.34 Constructing a Search with Boolean Operators

Searching in some online databases requires the use of "Boolean operators" (AND, OR, NOT), named for nineteenth-century logician George Boole. This guide contains explanations and examples of Boolean searching.

AND	**OR**	**NOT**
Both words must be present.	Either word, or both, should be present.	The word must not be present.
Makes the search more specific by requiring that *all* of your search words must be in the result; for example: **cats AND dogs**	Broadens the search. Best used for synonyms or like terms; for example: **cats OR felines** **IRS OR "internal revenue service"**	Helps to narrow the search by excluding some results; for example: **pets NOT cats**
On the web, AND is sometimes expressed as the menu option: Find results with *all of the words.*	On the web, OR is sometimes expressed as the menu option: Find results with *any of the words.*	On the web, NOT is sometimes expressed as the menu option: Find results with *none of the words.*
This search: **liberty AND death**	This search: **liberty OR death**	This search: **liberty NOT death**
Will find:	Will find:	Will find:
#1 Is life so dear, or peace so sweet, as to be purchased at the price of chains and slavery? Forbid it, Almighty God! I know not what course others may take; but as for me, give me **liberty** or give me **death**!	#1 Is life so dear, or peace so sweet, as to be purchased at the price of chains and slavery? Forbid it, Almighty God! I know not what course others may take; but as for me, give me **liberty** or give me **death**! #2 Four score and seven years ago our fathers brought forth on this continent a new nation, conceived in **liberty** and dedicated to the proposition that all men are created equal.	#2 Four score and seven years ago our fathers brought forth on this continent a new nation, conceived in **liberty** and dedicated to the proposition that all men are created equal.

✔ **Critically evaluate the results of your searches.** Can you identify the source of the information they provide? Is the information current and reasonably complete? Does the information lead to other promising sources?

§1.35 Searching and Limiting When You Get Too Much

The ideal search would find only information relevant to your information need and, if desired, all information relevant to your information need. Search tools are not sophisticated enough to achieve this, but various search techniques can help improve the usefulness of your search results.

✔ **Search on highly specific words and phrases.** Make your search terms as specific as possible. For example, "human anatomy" is more specific than "anatomy," which is more specific than "biology."

✔ **Limit your search to the most relevant section of the online offerings, if possible.** For example, searchers looking for a book on Amazon.com will be more efficient if they limit the search at the outset to just the "Books" section of Amazon.

✔ **Limit the parameters of your search, using the options on advanced search screens and elsewhere.** General search engines and other databases usually have options to limit your search results by language, type of document, publication date range, and other parameters. Specific examples follow.

§1.36 Dates

Use caution when limiting your search by publication date range. General search engines are often not able to distinguish true publication dates for web documents. Also, our recollections of when we saw a news article or heard a speech tend to be surprisingly inaccurate.

§1.37 Examples for Limiting When You Get Too Much

Library of Congress Online Catalog

The Library of Congress has voluminous collections of material in languages other than English. Also, many of the items in its catalog are not books, but maps, sound recordings, sheet music, etc. If you are interested in English-language books, select those limits from the outset. **❶**

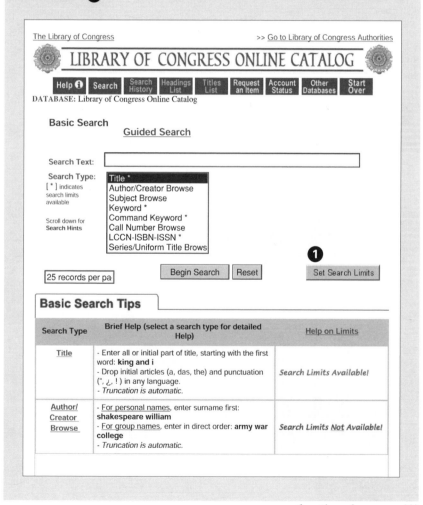

(continued on page 14)

§1.37 Examples for Limiting When You Get Too Much (continued)

The Federal Register

Each issue of the *Federal Register* includes many types of documents in addition to the announcement and printing of final regulations. To limit a search of the *Federal Register* on GPO Access *(<www.gpoaccess.gov/fr/>)* to final regulations, select that document type in the advanced search options. **2**

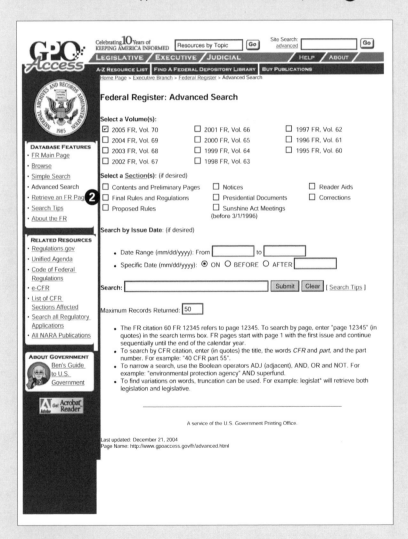

$1.38 Learn from the Pros

Experts from research and computer-related fields maintain web sites to track developments in search engines, test search engine performance, and develop resources and tutorials for search engine users. You can improve and keep your skills up-to-date by taking advantage of any of these expert sites:

ResearchBuzz

<www.researchbuzz.com>

ResearchBuzz provides fresh news about search engines, online databases, and other information resources.

The site is edited by Tara Calishain, author of several books on Internet searching.

Search Engine Watch

<http://searchenginewatch.com>

Search Engine Watch has resources for researchers as well as for those who want to list or advertise their sites on search engines. The Search Engine Listings section identifies leading and secondary search engines and news search engines. This is an excellent resource to check for alternative search engines to use.

The site is maintained by search engine consultants Danny Sullivan and Chris Sherman.

The Virtual Chase

<www.virtualchase.com>

The Virtual Chase specializes in legal Internet research news, but includes general information and web tutorials as well. In the legal area, the site is particularly strong on resources for finding and using public records online.

The Virtual Chase is owned by the law firm Ballard Spahr Andrews & Ingersoll, LLP, and edited by Genie Tyburski of that firm.

§1.40 Review Search Results Critically

So far, we have discussed finding information resources and conducting an online search. But the research process does not end there. Evaluating the information you have found is the next part of the story.

§1.41 Evaluating Information

✔ **What is the source of the information?** Is it readily identified? Does the source have any bias or motivation for bias? If the information is second-hand, find the original source.

✔ **Can the information be verified independently?** Find a second or third source to corroborate.

✔ **Is the information current?** If it may have been affected by newer developments, can you search for such news?

✔ **Is the information complete?** Think critically. You may never find "all" relevant information, but do you have the critical pieces you need for your purpose?

§1.42 Fact-Checking Resources

- The book *How to Lie with Statistics* (New York: W.W. Norton, 1993) is a classic, written in 1954 and reissued many times. It is a guide to understanding how others may use statistics in a misleading fashion.

- The **Public Agenda** web site *(<www.publicagenda.org>)* has a section about polling, with tips on critically evaluating poll results. The web site's Issue Guides section features "Red Flags" helpful in evaluating poll results for specific policy issues.

- The Annenberg Public Policy Center's **FactCheck.org** *(<www.factcheck.org>)* web site monitors, as they state, "the factual accuracy of what is said by major U.S. political players in the form of TV ads, debates, speeches, interviews, and news releases."

- **Snopes.com Urban Legend Reference Pages** *(<www.snopes.com>)* provides extensive background information on popular rumors, misinformation, strange news stories, and the type of fallacies or half-truths that travel quickly on the Internet.

§1.43 Evaluating a Web Site

✔ **Determine the author or sponsor of the web site.** Is the author clearly identified? Does the site provide information on its sponsor and how to contact them? Is the sponsor an individual or an institution? While there are exceptions to the rule, web sites sponsored by reputable institutions are generally more trustworthy than individual efforts. The institution must maintain its reputation and may have the resources to edit information for quality and accuracy. If you are not familiar with the identified author or sponsor, do further research.

✔ **Identify the purpose of the web site.** Is it clearly stated? Does it have a particular advocacy position or something to sell? Determine if the web site is non-partisan. Commercial, government, policy, political, and educational sites tend to have differing goals. This does not mean that the information one provides is any less worthy than the other, but you should be aware of the goals of the site or its sponsors.

§1.44 Web Tools for Evaluating Web Sites

Find out who links to the web site and what they say about it. Many search engines provide a feature, usually on the engine's advanced search page, that lets you find web sites that link to a specified site. The results can often provide clues about the site's popularity and whether reputable organizations find the site to be trustworthy.

Example on Google: link:www.hpol.org

Example on Yahoo!: link:http://www.hpol.org

"Whois" is an old Internet tool designed to provide information on who has registered a particular Internet web address, or domain. There are many "whois" tools available. Try Whois Source (*<www.whois.sc>*); it can search for information on web addresses in the .com, .net, .org, .info, .biz, and .us domains. Another to try is *<www.allwhois.com>*. Unfortunately, the accuracy and completeness of the domain registration information cannot be guaranteed—no matter which "whois" service you use—because it is up to the domain name owners themselves to provide the information.

✔ **Review the site's overall information quality.** Is information current? Check the date of the copyright statement and the currency of any press releases. Are links maintained? Is the source of information documented?

✔ **Assess the site's suitability to your research.** Does it have the required level of detail or the range of information needed? Does it appear to be a stable source you can refer to in the future?

✔ **Review the quality of the site's "web practices."** Does the web site follow good practices, such as not letting its own links go dead?

§1.50 Stay Informed

The Internet offers many ways to have information updates sent to you automatically. The sections below cover current awareness resources for information from and about government.

§1.51 Email Alert Services: A Selected Sample

The following free services deliver updates directly to your email account once you have requested a subscription.

- *Federal Register* table of contents. Subscribe via *<http://listserv. access.gpo.gov>*; click on "online mailing list archives," then look for FEDREGTOC-L.
- Public Laws Electronic Notification Service. Subscribe via *<www. archives.gov/federal-register/laws/updates.html>*. Notification of

§1.52 Avoid Information Overload

Too much information delivered to you automatically every day can be worse than none at all if it distracts from your primary mission, or if crucial data gets lost among the not-so-crucial data.

When you subscribe to a news update service or discussion list, learn how to unsubscribe and save the instructions for doing so.

Subscribe cautiously and weed subscriptions ruthlessly. Does the service duplicate news you get elsewhere? Is its coverage too broad in scope? Is there a more manageable source for the same information?

public law numbers as they are assigned by the National Archives Office of the Federal Register.

- *Whip Notice* and *Whipping Post* from House Majority Whip. Subscribe via *<http://majority whip.house.gov/Resources. asp>*. The weekly *Notice* lists bills expected to be considered in the upcoming week; the

Post lists bills expected to be considered that day. The House minority also offers whip notes at *<http://democraticwhip. house.gov>* for the House. Senate Majority Whip notices are not available via email but can be read at *<http://mcconnell.senate. gov/whip_office.cfm>*.

§1.54 Bloglines.com

Bloglines.com *<www.blog lines.com>* is a free web site that makes it easy to find and read blogs and RSS feeds *(see § 1.55)*. It features a list of the most popular blogs and has a searchable directory of blogs.

§1.53 Blogs: A Selected Sample

Blogs, short for "web logs," are web sites that are regularly updated with news or opinion. They usually consist of daily entries, with the most recent entries displayed prominently. The typical blog also has archived entries and links to related blogs. While many blogs deal in rumor or personal issues, the following examples provide useful information for the Washington researcher:

- beSpacific, *<www.bespacific.com>*, covers law and technology news. It is written by law librarian Sabrina Pacifici.
- ResourceShelf's DocuTicker, *<www.docuticker.com>*, announces new studies and reports from government agencies, foundations, think tanks, and other organizations. It is compiled by a team of research librarians.
- SCOTUSblog, *<www.scotusblog.com>*, reports on the U.S. Supreme Court. It is sponsored by Washington, DC, law firm Goldstein & Howe, P.C.

§1.55 RSS: A Selected Sample

RSS stands for "Really Simple Syndication," a format for information distribution. News services, government agencies, and other publishers are increasing their use of RSS for distribution of news updates independent of email. RSS news feeds are often indicated by an orange "XML" icon on the web page. Examples can be found at the following sites:

- Consumer Product Safety Commission provides an RSS feed of product recalls and safety news via *<www.cpsc.gov/cpscpub/prerel/prerel.html>*.
- State Department press briefings, press releases, and other updates are available via RSS at *<www.state.gov/misc/52620.htm>*.
- Yahoo! News, *<http://dailynews.yahoo.com>*, offers news feeds by category, such as politics or science news. Users can also create a customized news feed based on a word search. Yahoo! offers detailed information at *<http://news.yahoo.com/rss>*.

The federal government's FirstGov.gov site provides a directory of government RSS feeds at *<www.firstgov.gov/Topics/Reference_Shelf/Libraries/RSS_Library.shtml>*.

§1.56 Commercial Online Services

Many commercial online information services provide the ability to receive customized news updates. The services typically require a subscription. For more information, contact the companies directly. Online services providing such capabilities include:

- CQ.com, *<www.cq.com>*, for legislative news.
- GalleryWatch, *<www.gallerywatch.com>*, for legislative news.
- LexisNexis, *<www.lexisnexis.com>*, for a wide range of business, legal, and government news.
- Westlaw, *<http://west.thomson.com/store/>*, for a wide range of business, legal, and government news.

§1.60 **Remember, It's Not All Online**

Much of the world's knowledge cannot be found in online databases. Your research will often involve talking to experts and insiders (see Chapter 6) and can still involve traveling around town to use paper records.

§1.61 We Have So Many Records That . . .

The National Archives has created this cartoon to illustrate the fact that most of its records cannot be found online:

We have so many records that...

Laid side to side, pages in our holdings would circle the Earth over 57 times! Because of the cost to digitize such a volume of materials, **only a small percentage is available for research online.** Our web site offers tools and guides to help you locate these documents. To complete your research and use the records, you may need to <u>visit us</u>.

Source: <*www.archives.gov/research/*>

Chapter 2

Legislative Branch Research

The information resources of the legislative branch consist primarily of the documents of the U.S. Congress. THOMAS (*<http://thomas.loc.gov>*) and GPO Access (*<www.gpoaccess.gov>*), along with the web sites of the House (*<www.house.gov>*) and Senate (*<www.senate.gov>*), are the major congressional online services available to the public for free.

The following section has information about basic legislative resources, along with quick reference information related to legislative research. For further reading and much more information on legislative research resources, see *Congressional Deskbook* (Alexandria, VA: TheCapitol.Net, 2005).

§2.00 Legislative Process Flowchart

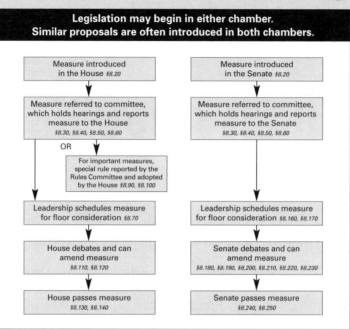

**Legislation may begin in either chamber.
Similar proposals are often introduced in both chambers.**

Measure introduced
in the House *§8.20*

Measure introduced
in the Senate *§8.20*

Measure referred to committee,
which holds hearings and reports
measure to the House
§8.30, §8.40, §8.50, §8.60

Measure referred to committee,
which holds hearings and reports
measure to the Senate
§8.30, §8.40, §8.50, §8.60

OR

For important measures,
special rule reported by the
Rules Committee and adopted
by the House *§8.90, §8.100*

Leadership schedules measure
for floor consideration *§8.70*

Leadership schedules measure
for floor consideration *§8.160, §8.170*

House debates and can
amend measure
§8.110, §8.120

Senate debates and can
amend measure
§8.180, §8.190, §8.200, §8.210, §8.220, §8.230

House passes measure
§8.130, §8.140

Senate passes measure
§8.240, §8.250

**Measures must pass both the House and the Senate
in identical form before being presented to the President.**

One chamber
agrees to the
other chamber's
version *§8.260*

OR

Each chamber appoints Members
to a conference committee, which
reconciles differences and agrees
to a conference report *§8.280*

OR

House and Senate
exchange amendments
to bill and reach
agreement *§8.270*

House approves conference report

Senate approves conference report

Legislation presented to the President.

President
signs
measure

If President does not
sign measure into law
within 10 days *§8.290*

President
vetoes
measure

Measure
becomes law

If Congress is
in session,
measure
becomes law

If Congress is not in
session, measure
does not become
law ("pocket veto")

Measure does not
become law, unless
both chambers override
veto by 2/3 majority

This chart is from, and section references are to, the *Congressional Deskbook* by Judy Schneider and Michael
Koempel. Copyright ©2005 by TheCapitol.Net, Inc. All Rights Reserved. 202-678-1600 www.TheCapitol.Net

§2.10 Quick Reference for Legislative Researchers

§2.11 Types of Legislation

Type	Abbreviation	Brief Description
Simple Resolution	H.Res., S.Res.	Used for administrative matters affecting only the House or only the Senate. Does not go to the other chamber or to the president. Does not have force of law. (The House also uses the H.Res. form for special rules from the Rules Committee.)
Concurrent Resolution	H.Con.Res., S.Con.Res.	Used for administrative matters affecting both chambers. Requires both chambers' approval but not signature of president. Does not have force of law.
Joint Resolution	H.J.Res., S.J.Res.	Similar to a bill, but used for specific purposes, such as proposed amendments to the Constitution. Requires the approval of both chambers and the president. If approved, has the force of law.
Bill	H.R., S.	Legislative proposal requiring approval of both chambers and the president to become law.
Amendment	H.Amdt., S.Amdt.	Text proposed by a member of Congress to change the text of legislation under consideration.

§2.12 Continuing Resolutions

When Congress fails to approve all appropriations bills before the end of the government's fiscal year each October 1, members will often pass what is referred to as a "continuing resolution" making temporary, continuing appropriations. A continuing resolution is not another type of bill. It is an unofficial term. These temporary measures typically are introduced as joint resolutions.

§2.13 Major Versions of Legislation

Version	Description
As Introduced	The initial version, when a bill or resolution number is assigned.
As Reported	The legislation as amended and reported favorably by committee to the House or Senate.
Engrossed	The legislation as passed by one chamber.
As Received in House As Received in Senate	The version of the legislation when it is accepted for consideration by one chamber or the other.
Enrolled	The final version as passed in identical form by both the House and Senate and sent to the president.

§2.14 Dates of Previous Congresses

A complete list of congressional session dates since 1789 is available from the Clerk of the House web site, at <*http://clerk.house. gov/histHigh/Congressional_History/Session_Dates/index.html*>.

Congress	Dates	Congress	Dates
109	2005–2006	101	1989–1990
108	2003–2004	100	1987–1988
107	2001–2002	99	1985–1986
106	1999–2000	98	1983–1984
105	1997–1998	97	1981–1982
104	1995–1996	96	1979–1980
103	1993–1994	95	1977–1978
102	1991–1992	94	1975–1976

§2.15 Legislative Glossaries

- **Congressional Bills: Glossary**
  <www.gpoaccess.gov/bills/glossary.html>
  Lists and explains the types and versions of legislation.

- **Congressional and Legislative Terms**
  <www.thecapitol.net/glossary/>
  Provides an extensive glossary of terms, from "act" to "veto" and beyond.

§2.20 Documents on THOMAS and GPO Access

THOMAS and GPO Access both provide access to the basic documents listed in the table below, albeit in different formats and for different time spans. For current committee hearings, check the committee home pages on the House and Senate web sites; GPO Access provides an incomplete selection of these from 1997 to present, and THOMAS does not have its own hearings database.

For more information, see TheCapitol.Net guide at *<congressional documents.com>*. For a more detailed listing of congressional documents online that includes commercial online services, see "Federal Legislative History Documents," by Richard J. McKinney of the Law Librarians' Society of Washington, DC, at *<www.llsdc.org/sourcebook/docs/elec-leg-hist-docs.pdf>*.

Content Highlights	THOMAS *<http://thomas.loc.gov>*	GPO Access *<www.gpoaccess.gov>*
Committee Reports	1995–present	1995–present
Congressional Record	1989–present	1994–present
Legislative status steps	1973–present	1983–present *(less detail, less current than THOMAS)*
Text of legislation	1989–present	1993–present
Text of public laws	*(THOMAS links to GPO for public laws)*	1995–present

§2.30 **THOMAS: Legislative Information on the Internet**

<http://thomas.loc.gov>

Scope:

- Summaries and status of legislation, 93rd Congress (1973–1974) to present.
- Full text of legislation (all versions of all bills), 101st Congress (1989–1990) to present.
- *Congressional Record*, full text, 101st Congress (1989–1990) to present.
- Roll call votes, 101st Congress (1989–1990) to present; House votes start with 1990.
- Committee reports (House, Senate, Joint & Conference), 104th Congress (1995–1996) to present.
- Links to related information, such as the House and Senate floor schedules and committee web sites.
- Charts tracking activity on appropriations legislation (best for Fiscal Year 2002 to present).
- Status of presidential nominations and treaties sent to the Senate for consideration.

Sponsor:

Library of Congress, on behalf of U.S. Congress. (Information in THOMAS is drawn from sources including the House, Senate, Government Printing Office, and Congressional Research Service.)

Description:

The Bill Summary and Status (BSS) database on THOMAS serves as the starting point for finding bills and amendments, and for finding information and documents related to a specific bill—such as debate in the *Congressional Record*, roll call votes, rules under which a bill was considered, and committee reports. BSS has a summary of each bill, written by the Congressional Research Service; a status section tracking the steps the bill has taken in the legislative process; and links to any closely related bills or amendments. **BSS is found under Bills and Resolutions.**

The Bill Text database on THOMAS allows you to search on every word in a bill. Bills found in this database also link to the complementary information available in the Bill Summary and Status database. **Bill Text is found under Bills and Resolutions.**

Other databases on THOMAS, such as the *Congressional Record*, are useful when looking for content that is not necessarily linked to a known bill.

THOMAS Tips:

- Most THOMAS databases are updated within twenty-four to forty-eight hours.
- The *Congressional Record* can be particularly difficult to search. If the date is known, try "Browse Daily Issues." To search by topic or a person's name, use "Keyword Index." Note: the Index has a two-week delay.
- When researching appropriations legislation, it is usually faster to go directly to the Appropriations Bills chart rather than search in other THOMAS databases. See § 2.40.
- Bill Text provides copies of bills in an HTML outline format. It links to "GPO's PDF" (an Adobe Acrobat format copy from the Government Printing Office) that is formatted like the print copy and can be easier to read. It also links to a "Printer Friendly" display, the full bill in HTML format, which can be easier to bring into word-processing programs.
- The Bill Summary and Status and Bill Text databases do not include the *public law* version of a bill. Instead, they carry all versions of the bill as it progresses, up to and including the *enrolled* version. The enrolled version is the version sent to the president for signature. The public law version adds the public law number, *Statutes at Large* citation, and date signed into law. To find the full text of the public law version, use the Public Laws database on THOMAS.

Word Searching:

- THOMAS will automatically search for information in which your search words appear exactly as you typed them. There is no need to use "quotes" to indicate a phrase.
- THOMAS will also show you results in which all of your search words appear, no matter the order.
- The advanced search screens for Bill Text and for Bill Summary and Status allow you to select whether you want to search for the words as you typed them or to also search for "variants" of those words. For example, if "variants" is selected, your search on *tax* will also find any occurrences of *taxes, taxing,* or *taxation.*

When searching THOMAS to:	Use:
• Get information about a bill • Track progress of a bill • Find bills sponsored by a certain member of Congress • Find a bill number when you have some information (for example, sponsor and topic of the bill) • Get a list of vetoed bills	Summary and Status Information See § 2.32 ❷
• Get a copy of a bill when you know the bill number • Search the full text of bills	Bill Text See § 2.32 ❶
• Get a committee report, when report number is known • Get a committee report, when the number of the reported bill is known	Committee Reports See § 2.31 ❷
• Find *Congressional Record* statements on a bill	Summary and Status Information (status links to *Congressional Record*) See § 2.32 ❷
• Find *Congressional Record* statements on a topic	*Congressional Record* See § 2.31 ❸

§2.31 Thomas Home Page

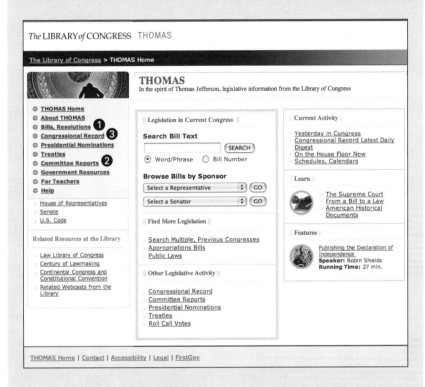

❶ To search Bills and Resolutions

❷ To search Committee Reports

❸ To search the Congressional Record

§2.32 Thomas Bills and Resolutions Search Page

The LIBRARY *of* CONGRESS   THOMAS

The Library of Congress > THOMAS Home > Bills, Resolutions

Bills, Resolutions

- THOMAS Home
- About THOMAS
- Bills, Resolutions
- Congressional Record
- Presidential Nominations
- Treaties
- Committee Reports
- Government Resources
- For Teachers
- Help

  › House of Representatives
  › Senate
  › U.S. Code

Related Resources at the Library

  › Law Library of Congress
  › Century of Lawmaking
  › Continental Congress and
    Constitutional Convention
  › Related Webcasts from the
    Library

Search Bill Text | Search Bill Summary, Status | Search Multiple Congresses

THOMAS provides many options for finding legislation and information about legislation. These options are described below.

Search Bill Text

Search the full text of legislation for words or phrases or search by bill number.

Coverage: The Bill Text feature covers the 101st Congress (1989) to the current Congress. Users must select the Congress that they would like to search.

Search Bill Text

Search Bill Summary & Status

Bill Summary & Status (BSS) contains information **about** bills and amendments. Whereas the Bill Text feature (described above) searches the full text of legislation, the BSS feature searches everything but the actual text of the legislation. The BSS information includes: sponsor(s); cosponsor(s); official, short and popular titles; floor/executive actions; detailed legislative history; Congressional Record page references; bill summary; committee information; amendment information; subjects (indexing terms assigned to each bill); a link to the full text versions of the bill; and if the bill has been enacted into law, a link to the full text of the law on the Government Printing Office Web site.

Coverage: BSS covers the 93rd Congress (1973) through the current Congress. Users must select the Congress that they would like to search

Search Bill Summary & Status

Advanced Search

Search Multiple Congresses

The full text of legislation can be searched across multiple Congresses.

Coverage: The full text of legislation from the 101st (1989) through the current Congress can be searched at the same time. Users can select one or more Congresses to search.

Search Multiple Congresses

THOMAS Home | Contact | Accessibility | Legal | FirstGov

❶ To search the full text of Bills and Resolutions

❷ To search only the Summary Abstracts and Status
   of Bills and Resolutions

§2.40 Appropriations Legislation

In each session of each Congress, appropriations bills are some of the most complex and most closely watched legislation. Your research is made much easier by a chart maintained on the THOMAS web site. See the partial sample below for an example for Fiscal Year 2003. For Fiscal Year 2006, go to *<http://thomas.loc.gov/home/approp/app06.html>*.

The LIBRARY *of* CONGRESS   THOMAS

The Library of Congress > THOMAS Home > Appropriations > Status of Appropriations Legislation for Fiscal Year 2003

Status of Appropriations Legislation for Fiscal Year 2003

Appropriations Legislation for Fiscal Year: 2006 | 2005 | 2004 | 2003 | 2002 | 2001 | 2000 | 1999 | 1998

SIGNED INTO LAW: Defense, Military Construction, Omnibus (incorporates the 11 non-defense bills), & Wartime Supplemental

Updated July 5, 2005

Appropriations	House Approvals			Senate Approvals			Conference Approvals			Public Law
	Committee Report	Comm. Vote	House Vote	Committee Report	Comm. Vote	Senate Vote	Conf. Report	House Vote	Senate Vote	
Wartime Supplemental Appropriations HR1559 S762	H.Rpt. 108-55	04/01/03 59-0	04/03/03 rc	S.Rpt. 108-33	04/01/03	S762: 04/03/03 rc HR1559: 04/07/03 uc	H.Rpt. 108-76 Highlights	04/12/03 vv	04/12/03 uc	PL108-11 04/16/03
Omnibus Appropriations 108th: H.J.Res. 2			01/28/03 uc agreed to conference			01/23/03 rc	H.Rpt. 108-10 Summary	02/13/03 rc	02/13/03 rc	PL108-7 02/20/03
Note: HJRes2 was approved in the House as a continuing resolution; the Senate amended it with a substitute, S.Amdt. 1, incorporating 11 non-defense bills. Additional amendments were also adopted.										
Agriculture HR5263 S2801	H.Rpt. 107-623	07/11/02		S.Rpt. 107-223	07/25/02					
Commerce/Justice/State S2778 108th: HR247				S.Rpt. 107-218	07/18/02					
Defense HR5010 Senate Comm	H.Rpt. 107-532 vv	06/24/02	06/27/02 rc	S.Rpt. 107-213	07/18/02	08/01/02 rc	H.Rpt. 107-732	10/10/02 rc	10/16/02 rc	PL107-248 10/23/02
District of Columbia HR5521 S2809	H.Rpt. 107-716	09/26/02		S.Rpt. 107-225	07/25/02					
Energy & Water HR5431 S2784	H.Rpt. 107-681	09/05/02		S.Rpt. 107-220	07/24/02					
Foreign Operations HR5410 S2779	H.Rpt. 107-663	09/19/02		S.Rpt. 107-219	07/18/02					
Interior HR5093 S2708	H.Rpt. 107-564	07/09/02	07/17/02 rc	S.Rpt. 107-201	06/27/02 (29-0)					
Labor/HHS/ Education HR5320 S2766 108th: HR246				S.Rpt. 107-216	07/18/02					
Legislative Branch HR5121 S2720	H.Rpt. 107-576	07/11/02	07/18/02 rc	S.Rpt. 107-209	07/11/02	07/25/02 rc				
Military Construction HR5011 S2709	H.Rpt. 107-533 vv	06/24/02	06/27/02 rc	S.Rpt. 107-202	06/27/02	07/18/02 rc	H.Rpt. 107-731	10/10/02 rc	10/11/02 uc	PL107-249 10/23/02
Transportation HR5559 S2808	H.Rpt. 107-722	10/01/02		S.Rpt. 107-224	07/25/02					
Treasury/Postal HR5120 S2240	H.Rpt. 107-575	07/09/02	07/24/02 rc	S.Rpt. 107-212	07/16/02					
VA/HUD HR5605 S2797	H.Rpt. 107-740	10/09/02		S.Rpt. 107-222	07/25/02					
1st Continuing Resolution H.J.Res. 111		09/25/02	09/26/02 rc			09/26/02 uc				PL107-229 09/30/02
2nd Continuing Resolution H.J.Res. 112			10/03/02 rc			10/03/02 uc				PL107-235 10/04/02
3rd Continuing Resolution H.J.Res. 120										
4th Continuing Resolution H.J.Res. 121										
5th Continuing Resolution H.J.Res. 122			10/10/02 rc			10/11/02 uc				PL107-240 10/11/02

§2.41 Appropriations Committees and Subcommittees

Appropriations bills are crafted by the House and Senate Appropriations Committees and their subcommittees. Further information on committee membership and jurisdiction is available from the House Appropriations Committee web site (*<http://appropriations.house.gov>*) and the Senate Appropriations Committee web site (*<http://appropriations.senate.gov>*).

New Appropriations Subcommittee Organization

Congress annually considers regular appropriations bills to provide budget authority to agencies for the upcoming fiscal year. Each regular appropriations bill typically has been developed by the relevant House and Senate Appropriations subcommittee. At the beginning of the 109th Congress, the House and Senate Appropriations Committees reorganized their subcommittees, with the House eliminating three subcommittees and the Senate Appropriations Committee eliminating one. The subcommittee organization and the resulting regular appropriations bills will no longer be parallel and thus will require some resolution when the two committees resolve any differences before sending the measures to the president. The Appropriations subcommittees of the House and Senate are the following:

House	Senate
Agriculture, Rural Development, Food and Drug Administration, and Related Agencies	Agriculture, Rural Development, and Related Agencies
Defense	Defense
Energy and Water Development, and Related Agencies	Energy and Water, and Related Agencies
Foreign Operations, Export Financing, and Related Agencies	State, Foreign Operations, and Related Programs
Department of Homeland Security	Homeland Security
Interior, Environment, and Related Agencies	Interior and Related Agencies
Departments of Labor, Health and Human Services, Education, and Related Agencies	Labor, Health and Human Services, Education, and Related Agencies
Military Quality of Life and Veterans Affairs, and Related Agencies	Military Construction and Veterans Affairs, and Related Agencies
Science, the Departments of State, Justice, and Commerce, and Related Agencies	Commerce, Justice, Science, and Related Agencies
Departments of Transportation, Treasury, and Housing and Urban Development, the Judiciary, District of Columbia, and Independent Agencies	Transportation, Treasury, the Judiciary, Housing and Urban Development, and Related Agencies
	District of Columbia
Legislative Branch [no subcommittee, handled by full committee]	Legislative Branch

From § 9.82, *Congressional Deskbook*, *<CongressionalDeskbook.com>*

§2.42 Appropriations Conference Committee Reports

In order for a bill to be sent to the president for his approval or veto, the House and Senate must pass the bill in identical form. For most complex legislation, Congress uses a conference committee to resolve differences between the House and Senate versions. The regular appropriations bills are particularly complex measures, and they almost always go through a conference committee. (See the legislative process flowchart at § 2.00 for the place of the conference committee in the legislative process.)

Conference committees issue their agreement in what is commonly referred to as a "conference report." In fact, this document is a combination of two distinct documents: the conference report and the conference managers' statement (also called the joint explanatory statement). Togeth-

§2.43 Limitations, Earmarks, and General Provisions

In addition to appropriating specific dollar amounts, appropriations and their accompanying reports contain numerous other provisions that affect how federal departments and agencies spend appropriations. The principal categories of these provisions include the following:

- **Limitation**—language in legislation or in legislative documents that restricts the availability of an appropriation by limiting its use or amount.

- **Earmark**—a set-aside within an appropriation for a specific purpose that might be included either in legislation or in legislative documents.

- **Directive**—an instruction, probably in a legislative document, to an agency concerning the manner in which an appropriation is to be administered.

- **General Provision**—policy guidance on spending included in an appropriations measure; it may affect some or all appropriation accounts in the measure or even have government-wide application; it may also be one-time or permanent.

Appropriations measures might also contain *riders,* legislative provisions that are included in appropriations measures despite House and Senate rules discouraging the practice.

From § 9.81, *Congressional Deskbook, <CongressionalDeskbook.com>*

er, these two documents are properly referred to as the "conference papers." The report contains the negotiated legislative language, while the managers' statement is a plain English explanation of each part of the agreement.

The managers' statement is particularly important for legislative researchers because it may contain provisions that are not included in the actual text of the appropriations bill. For example, the managers' statement in the conference papers (H.Rpt. 109-188) for the Interior-Environment-Related Agencies 2006 appropriations bill (H.R. 2361, 109th Cong.) spells out that $640,000 of the appropriations are to be used for re-striping and sealing the Natchez Trace Parkway; the Parkway is not specifically mentioned in the language of the bill.

§ 2.43 provides more information on special provisions that may or may not appear in the text of the legislation.

§2.50 Tracking and Monitoring Legislation: Alert Services

Free and paid subscription alert services can be used to automatically monitor databases, news sources, and web sites and deliver any updates to the subscriber. Typically, the updates are delivered to the subscriber's email account. A relatively new format is RSS (Really Simple Syndication, see § 1.55), which allows subscribers to receive updates independent of an email account. Instead, updates can be viewed with RSS news reader software, on the web, or on a handheld communication device.

The following selective list of alert services focuses on tracking and monitoring legislation and policy developments.

Congressional Sources
Leadership and Committees

- *Whip Notice* and *Whipping Post* are available from the House Majority Whip. Subscribe via *<http://majoritywhip.house.gov/Resources.asp>*. The weekly *Notice* lists bills expected to be considered in the upcoming week; the *Post* lists bills expected to be considered that day.
- *Daily Whip* and *Weekly Whip* are issued by the House Democratic Whip. Subscribe via *<http://democraticwhip.house.gov/whip/daily.cfm>*.

- The Senate Majority Whip *Daily Whip Notice* is not available for email but can be viewed at *<http://mcconnell.senate.gov/whip_ office.cfm>*.
- Some committee web sites provide email alert services via the committee home page. The offerings vary from committee to committee, but they often include schedule updates and press releases. Some provide alerts limited to a specific topic or topics covered by the committee.

Congressional Agencies

- The Congressional Budget Office (CBO) alert service notifies subscribers about new CBO reports. Subscribe via *<www.cbo. gov/pubs_index.cfm>*.
- The Government Accountability Office (GAO) provides several email alert services, all available via *<www.gao.gov/subtest/*

§2.51 Recorded Congressional Information

Some congressional and related information is regularly updated on telephone recordings.

House of Representatives Floor Schedule Information:
Democratic Recording (advance schedule), 202-225-1600
Democratic Recording (current proceedings), 202-225-7400
Republican Recording (advance schedule), 202-225-2020
Republican Recording (current proceedings), 202-225-7430

Senate Floor Schedule Information:
Democratic Recording, 202-224-8541
Republican Recording, 202-224-8601

Government Printing Office:
New Congressional Publications, 202-512-1809

White House Executive Clerk:
Status of Bills Received, 202-456-2226

Office of the Federal Register:
New Public Law Numbers, 202-741-6043

From § 11.15, *Congressional Deskbook*, *<CongressionalDeskbook.com>*

subscribe.html>. The daily and monthly alert services send email messages with links to GAO reports and testimony released in the previous day or over the course of the past month. Subscribers can also choose to receive alerts only when the content is related to a selected topic, such as homeland security or veterans' affairs. GAO offers an RSS feed as well.

Commercial Sources (paid subscription services)

- CQ.com, *<www.cq.com>*, provides alert services with legislative news, analysis, and documents.
- GalleryWatch.com, *<www.gallerywatch.com>*, has a Legislative Tracking and Notification Service.
- LexisNexis, *<www.lexisnexis.com>*, and Westlaw, *<http://west. thomson.com>*, each carry legislative databases such as the *Congressional Record*, and each offer alert services.

§2.60 From Bills to Laws: Documents and Information Resources

Legislation is introduced, debated, amended, and passed by Congress.

The final version of legislation, the enrolled bill, is sent to the president.

Resources:

- THOMAS, *<http://thomas.loc.gov>*
- GPO Access, *<www.gpoaccess.gov/bills/>*

Legislation is signed into law by the president.

The White House sends the signed copy to the National Archives, Office of the Federal Register (OFR). The National Archives assigns a public law number and the Government Printing Office (GPO) prints the bill as a public law, or "slip law."

Resources:

- National Archives, OFR, *<www.archives.gov/federal-register/laws/>*
- GPO Access, *<www.gpoaccess.gov/plaws/>*

(continued on page 39)

§2.60 From Bills to Laws:
Documents and Information Resources (continued)

**Public laws are compiled chronologically
for *Statutes At Large* volumes.**

The annual volumes are compiled by the OFR and printed by
the GPO. Current volumes are not yet available on a free web site,
although GPO plans to put some volumes online in the near future.
They are available for sale from GPO or can be used at a local GPO
Federal Depository Library.

Resources:

- GPO Online Bookstore, *<http://bookstore.gpo.gov>*
- GPO Federal Depository Library Directory,
  <www.gpoaccess.gov/libraries.html>

(Laws are also compiled in the commercially published *United States
Code Congressional and Administrative News* from Thomson-West,
<http://west.thomson.com>.)

**Public laws of a "general and permanent" nature
are compiled by topic for the United States Code.**

The Law Revision Counsel of the House of Representatives assigns
law text to the Code's topical hierarchy. The official *U.S. Code* is
published by GPO every six years, within interim supplements.
Many researchers prefer to use unofficial versions that are
published commercially on such for-fee online services as
Westlaw, *<http://west.thomson.com/store/>*, or free services
such as Cornell University's Legal Information Institute.

Resources:

- House Law Revision Counsel, *<http://uscode.house.gov/>*
- GPO Access, *<www.gpoaccess.gov/uscode/>*
- Cornell Legal Information Institute,
  <www.law.cornell.edu/uscode/>

(The Code is also published commercially as the *United States Code
Annotated*, from Thomson-West, *<http://west.thomson.com>*, and the
United States Code Service, from LexisNexis, *<www.lexisnexis.com>*).

**The United States Code is continually amended
as new bills are signed into law.**

§2.70 United States Code Titles

"The United States Code (USC) is the codification by subject matter of the general and permanent laws of the United States. It is divided by broad subjects into 50 titles and published by the Office of the Law Revision Counsel of the U.S. House of Representatives. Since 1926, the United States Code has been published every six years. In between editions, annual cumulative supplements are published in order to present the most current information."

—Government Printing Office, *<www.gpoaccess.gov/uscode/>*

The *United States Code* is available online for free at several web sites, including:

- GPO Access, at *<www.gpoaccess.gov/uscode/>*
- Cornell's Legal Information Institute, at *<www.law.cornell.edu/uscode/>*

USC Titles

Title 1	General Provisions
Title 2	The Congress
Title 3	The President
Title 4	Flag and Seal, Seat of Government, and the States
Title 5	Government Organization and Employees; and Appendix
Title 6	Domestic Security
Title 7	Agriculture
Title 8	Aliens and Nationality
Title 9	Arbitration
Title 10	Armed Forces; and Appendix
Title 11	Bankruptcy; and Appendix
Title 12	Banks and Banking
Title 13	Census
Title 14	Coast Guard
Title 15	Commerce and Trade
Title 16	Conservation
Title 17	Copyrights
Title 18	Crimes and Criminal Procedure; and Appendix

(continued on page 41)

USC Titles (continued)

Title 19	Customs Duties
Title 20	Education
Title 21	Food and Drugs
Title 22	Foreign Relations and Intercourse
Title 23	Highways
Title 24	Hospitals and Asylums
Title 25	Indians
Title 26	Internal Revenue Code; and Appendix
Title 27	Intoxicating Liquors
Title 28	Judiciary and Judicial Procedure; and Appendix
Title 29	Labor
Title 30	Mineral Lands and Mining
Title 31	Money and Finance
Title 32	National Guard
Title 33	Navigation and Navigable Waters
Title 34	Navy (Repealed)
Title 35	Patents
Title 36	Patriotic Societies and Observances
Title 37	Pay and Allowances of the Uniformed Services
Title 38	Veterans' Benefits; and Appendix
Title 39	Postal Service
Title 40	Public Buildings, Property, and Works; and Appendix
Title 41	Public Contracts
Title 42	The Public Health and Welfare
Title 43	Public Lands
Title 44	Public Printing and Documents
Title 45	Railroads
Title 46	Shipping; and Appendix
Title 47	Telegraphs, Telephones, and Radiotelegraphs
Title 48	Territories and Insular Possessions
Title 49	Transportation
Title 50	War and National Defense; and Appendix

§2.80 Additional Legislative Branch Sources

§2.81 Congressional Research Service
Reports and Issue Briefs

The Congressional Research Service, <*www.loc.gov/crsinfo/*>, a nonpartisan congressional support agency located within the Library of Congress, provides Congress with independent policy research and analysis. CRS prepares reports, issue briefs, memos, online information, and other information products exclusively for Congress. CRS products are not distributed directly to the public, although the public can request copies from their representatives in Congress.

Because CRS policy papers are not freely and directly available to the public, various for-profit and nonprofit organizations have developed services to obtain and distribute them. For further information, see the excellent article "CRS Reports," by Stephen Young, at <*www.llrx.com/features/crsreports.htm*>. Since the article was written, one other service has appeared: OpenCRS, <*http://www.opencrs.com*>, sponsored by the Center for Democracy & Technology.

§2.82 Lobbyist Registrations

Lobbyists are required to register with the chamber—House, Senate, or both—that they are lobbying. The Senate Office of Public Records makes images of the files available on its web site at <*http://sopr.senate.gov/*>. Because many lobbyists register with both chambers, the Senate site may provide all of the information you need. House records must be accessed on-site, at the House Legislative Resource Center, B-106 Cannon House Office Building in Washington, DC. See also § 4.21, "Resources on Lobbying," *Congressional Deskbook*.

Chapter 3

Judicial Branch Research

Legal research is a specialized practice that involves an understanding of the area of law being researched as well as the tools being used. Advanced legal research often requires the use of commercial online services such as the law firm standards LexisNexis (commonly misspelled "LexusNexus"), *<www.lexisnexis.com>*, and Westlaw, *<http://west.thomson.com/>*, or other paid-subscription resources such as Loislaw.com and Versuslaw.com. For the limited research that those outside the legal professions may need to do, free web sites such as FindLaw.com and the various court and law library web sites may suffice.

TheCapitol.Net also has a page of links to legal resources, "Legal Reference and Research Tools," at *<www.thecapitol.net/Research/legalFTL.htm>*.

This section provides basic information on the federal courts, judiciary, and useful web sites for non-specialists.

§3.00 Federal Court System Structure

Supreme Court	United States Supreme Court (commonly abbreviated as SCOTUS) <*www.supremecourtus.gov*>
Appellate courts	United States Courts of Appeal <*www.uscourts.gov/courtlinks*> —Includes twelve regional courts of appeal and the Court of Appeals for the Federal Circuit
Trial courts	United States District Courts <*www.uscourts.gov/courtlinks*> —Includes ninety-four judicial districts and the United States Bankruptcy Courts Court of International Trade <*www.cit.uscourts.gov*> Court of Federal Claims <*www.uscfc.uscourts.gov*>
Other federal tribunals that are not within the judicial branch	Military courts (trial and appellate) United States Court of Veterans Appeals <*www.vetapp.gov*> United States Tax Court <*www.ustaxcourt.gov*> Administrative agency offices and boards (A useful list of links is compiled by the University of Virginia Library at <*www.lib.virginia.edu/govdocs/fed_decisions_agency.html*>)

§3.10 Regional Federal Court Circuits— Geographic Coverage

(All federal circuit court web addresses are at
<www.uscourts.gov/courtlinks>.)

Circuit	Geographic Coverage
First	Maine, Massachusetts, New Hampshire, Puerto Rico, Rhode Island
Second	Connecticut, New York, Vermont
Third	Delaware, New Jersey, Pennsylvania, U.S. Virgin Islands
Fourth	Maryland, North Carolina, South Carolina, Virginia, West Virginia
Fifth	Louisiana, Mississippi, Texas
Sixth	Kentucky, Michigan, Ohio, Tennessee
Seventh	Illinois, Indiana, Wisconsin
Eighth	Arkansas, Iowa, Minnesota, Missouri, Nebraska, North Dakota, South Dakota
Ninth	Alaska, Arizona, California, Guam, Hawaii, Idaho, Montana, Nevada, Northern Mariana Islands, Oregon, Washington
Tenth	Colorado, Kansas, New Mexico, Oklahoma, Utah, Wyoming
Eleventh	Alabama, Florida, Georgia
District of Columbia Circuit	Washington, DC
Federal Circuit	National jurisdiction. Hears appeals in specialized cases, such as those involving patent laws and cases decided by the Court of International Trade and the Court of Federal Claims.

§3.20 Sources of Supreme Court Opinions Online

Supreme Court of the United States

<www.supremecourtus.gov>

The Supreme Court's web site is the official online source for the Court's slip opinions. Opinions are available online for 2001 to present. Current opinions are posted to the web site in PDF format within hours after they are issued. Researchers can select an opinion from lists of opinions in date order. There is no word-search capability.

The Supreme Court site also has transcripts of *oral arguments* before the Court for the 2000 term to the present, with about a two-week delay.

FindLaw: Cases and Codes:
Supreme Court Opinions

<www.findlaw.com/casecode/supreme.html>

FindLaw is a web site owned by the West Group, which also owns the Westlaw online information service. FindLaw has a free, searchable database of all Supreme Court opinions since 1893. (The Court issued its first opinion in 1792.) Opinions on FindLaw can be searched by word, party name, and *U.S. Reports* citation[1].

FindLaw also has a section called Supreme Court Center. Among other resources, it includes copies of *legal briefs* filed in U.S. Supreme Court cases from 1999 to present and a subject index to opinions from the current term. FindLaw's Supreme Court Center is at *<http://supreme.lp. findlaw.com/supreme_court/resources.html>*.

Legal Information Institute
Supreme Court Collection

<www.law.cornell.edu/supct/>

Cornell University's online Legal Information Institute service has the searchable text of Supreme Court decisions from 1990 to present. In addition, it features a collection of over 600 important *historic decisions* from the Court's more than 200-year history. Under the heading Archive of Decisions, the opinions are sorted by topic, author, and party name.

---

1. Supreme Court opinions are cited by the volume and page number of the official *United States Reports* volume in which they appear; for example: 347 U.S. 483

Comparison of Supreme Court Opinion Sites

Web Site	Date Coverage	Word Search	Browse	Citation Search	Format(s)
Supreme Court <*www.supreme courtus.gov*>	2001 to present	No	Yes	No	PDF
FindLaw <*www.findlaw. com/casecode/ supreme.html*>	1893 to present	Yes	Yes	Yes	HTML
Legal Information Institute <*www.law.cornell. edu/supct/*>	1990 to present + historical selection	Yes	Yes	No	HTML PDF

§3.30 The Federal Courts: Selected Internet Resources

Courts and Opinions

- Administrative Office of the U.S. Courts
  <*www.uscourts.gov*>
  Links to all federal court sites and to educational information on the federal judiciary.

- Federal Law Materials—Judicial Opinions
  <*www.law.cornell.edu/federal/opinions.html*>
  Links and coverage notes for free, public web sites carrying federal judicial opinions.

- Georgetown University Law "Find It Fast" Page
  <*www.ll.georgetown.edu/find/*>
  Guides to the key books, databases, and web sites for a wide variety of legal topics.

Federal Judges

- Federal Judicial Vacancies
  <*www.uscourts.gov/judicialvac.html*>
  The Federal Judicial Conference tracks statistics on vacancies, nominations, and confirmations at this site.

- Judges of the United States Courts
  <*www.fjc.gov/history/home.nsf*>
  Biographies of federal judges from 1789 to present.

§3.40 Citing the Law

Legal professionals adhere to a standard style for citing legal and other information resources so the material can easily be found by others. Citations usually indicate the name of the legal source (abbreviated), the volume and page number(s), and date. For example, an opinion of the Supreme Court would be cited as *New York v. Quarles*, 467 U. S. 649 (1984). If a particular statement within the opinion is being cited, the citation would also include the official page number where that statement can be found, such as 467 U. S. 649, 655. Electronic sources often include the official pagination so that individual pages can be cited even if the document is not in book form.

§3.41 Citing Decisions at the Federal Level—Examples

Supreme Court:	*Brown v. Board of Education,* 347 U.S. 483 (1954)
Courts of Appeal:	*Reed v. Sullivan,* 988 F.2d 812, 816 (8th Cir. 1993)
	Culbertson v. Shalala, 30 F.3d 934 (8th Cir. 1994)
District Courts:	*Padilla v. Bush,* 233 F. Supp. 2d 564 (S.D.N.Y. 2002)
	South Dakota v. Adams, 506 F. Supp. 50 (D.S.D. 1980)

A good basic guide is available online. "Introduction to Basic Legal Citation," by Peter W. Martin can be consulted or downloaded in whole at *<www.law.cornell.edu/citation/index.htm>*. The guide includes examples for electronic resources, judicial opinions, public laws, regulations, and other document types.

The standard reference for legal citation is a book commonly referred to as "The Bluebook." The book, *The Bluebook: A Uniform System of Citation* (Cambridge, MA: The Harvard Law Review Association), is not available online but can found in print at many bookstores and libraries.

§3.50 FindLaw Legal Dictionary

<http://dictionary.lp.findlaw.com/>

The practice of law uses a specialized vocabulary. To help interpret the law, FindLaw offers this free dictionary of legal terms.

Chapter 4

Executive Branch Research

The executive branch includes the Executive Office of the President, fifteen departments, and numerous independent agencies, commissions, boards, and other entities. The official U.S. government web site, FirstGov (<*www.firstgov.gov*>), provides central access to the web resources of the executive branch, and also links to legislative and judicial branch sites.

This section includes information on using First-Gov and on finding the regulatory, administrative, and other resources of the executive branch.

§4.00 Executive Branch Organization

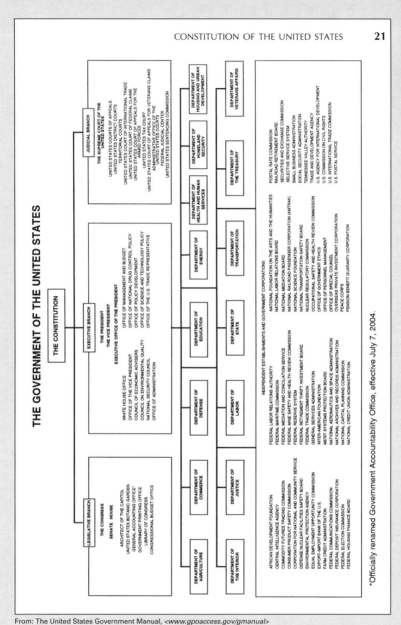

From: The United States Government Manual, <www.gpoaccess.gov/gmanual>

§4.10 FirstGov

<www.firstgov.gov>

Scope:

- Links to federal, state, local, and tribal government web sites and to nongovernment sites with government-related information.
- Search engine for federal and state government information on the web.
- Special sections for citizens, businesses and nonprofits, federal employees, and governments.
- Full Spanish-language version, linked from FirstGov home page.

Sponsor:

General Services Administration, on behalf of the White House and executive branch.

Description:

FirstGov describes itself as "the U.S. Government's Official Web Portal." The site is an interagency initiative supported by the White House and managed by the General Services Administration to provide organized access to U.S. government information.

FirstGov organizes links to government information by topic, audience, agency, and other schemes. The FirstGov search engine is a key feature.

This site is useful for finding government information when you do not know which agency will have it and for locating the URLs for government web sites.

FirstGov Search Engine Tips:

A **basic search** box is in the upper right corner of the home page. This searches the content on the FirstGov site and on many other government web sites. To search:

- Enter your search words.
- Review results, which are displayed in relevance-ranked order.

The **advanced search** screen allows you to set specific parameters to narrow your search. These include:

- Limiting to only English-language or only Spanish-language results.
- Limiting by file format, such as only PDF documents or only Microsoft PowerPoint files.

- Limiting your search to one, or several, specific government web sites.
- Limiting to only federal government sites, or to a specific state or all states.

No search engine is comprehensive. Try FirstGov along with alternatives, such as a relevant federal agency's web site or a general search engine.

Information for Researchers:

FirstGov has a number of sections to assist the Washington researcher. Most are grouped under Reference Center in the left-hand column. Click on "more" in this section to see the complete listing.

Highlights include:

- **Data and Statistics.** Links to the federal statistics gateway site, FedStats.gov, and to other federal statistical sites such as EconomicIndicators.gov and ChildStats.gov.
- **Graphics and Photos.** An index to government web pages that offer collections of graphics and photos, most of which can be downloaded. Most, but not all, government content is free of copyright restrictions. Review the disclaimer on FirstGov and at individual agency sites before downloading for re-use.
- **Laws and Regulations.** Links to federal and state web sites for laws, regulations, court directories, and related information. (*Tip: searchers may find nongovernment alternatives, such as Findlaw.com or the Legal Information Institute, at <www.law. cornell.edu>, to be more helpful.*)
- **News.** This section includes several useful links. "Federal Agency News and Press Releases" is an index to federal executive, legislative, and judicial branch web pages that include government news releases. The "Government Email Newsletters" page provides easy subscription access to a broad selection of free government email newsletters.

The "Phone" section under Contact Your Government, in the left-hand column of the FirstGov home page, is also useful for researchers. This section includes:

- **Federal Employee Phone Directories, by Agency.** Links to major government phone directories online, as well as to the individual agency phone directories online at agency sites.

FirstGov Tips:

The FirstGov site links to both government and nongovernment web sites that cover government-related topics. Be aware that most links take you off the FirstGov site. The link names themselves give no indication whether they lead to a government, educational, or commercial site. Check the sponsor or author of the content for each new site you reach through FirstGov.

FirstGov is a useful tool but, like many web sites, it may have broken or out-of-date links. FirstGov is best used to discover which government web sites cover a topic. Once those sites have been found, you may wish to explore them directly to find newer or more relevant content.

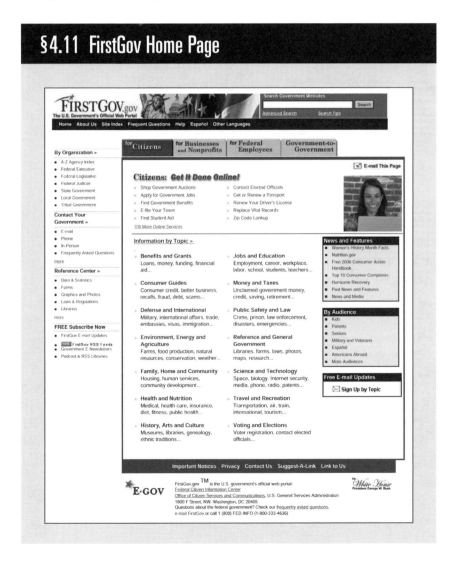

§4.11 FirstGov Home Page

§4.20 Sources for Presidential and Other White House Documents

§4.21 Presidential Documents on Government Web Sites

White House Web Site

<www.whitehouse.gov>

- Press releases
- Radio addresses
- Executive orders
- Proclamations
- Vice President's press releases
- Office of Management and Budget documents (see § 4.24 below).

National Archives

<www.archives.gov>

- Executive Order disposition tables, *<www.archives.gov/federal-register/executive-orders/disposition.html>*.
- Web sites for the libraries of former presidents, *<www.archives.gov/presidential-libraries/>*; includes guide to presidential documents online, *<www.archives.gov/presidential-libraries/research/guide.html>*.

GPO Access

<www.gpoaccess.gov/executive.html>

- Weekly Compilation of Presidential Documents (1993–)
- Public Papers of the Presidents (1991–2001, as of 2005)
- *Federal Register* (1995–current) and Title 3 of the *Code of Federal Regulations* for Executive Orders (1996–current)
- State of the Union Addresses (1992–)

§4.22 Presidential Documents on Nongovernment Web Sites

The American Presidency Project

<www.presidency.ucsb.edu>

- This project is building an extensive collection of current and historic documents. It also has information on presidential elections.

§4.23 President's Budget Documents

Volumes Containing and Explaining the President's Annual Budget

The principal volumes currently part of the president's annual budget submission include the following:

- **Budget** (officially the *Budget of the United States Government*)—includes the president's budget message, detailed presentations on the president's major budgetary initiatives, a descriptive discussion of federal programs organized by budget function, and summary tables.

- **Appendix**—sets forth detailed financial information on individual programs and appropriations accounts.

- **Analytical Perspectives**—contains analyses designed to highlight specified subject areas or provide other significant presentations of budget data that place the budget in perspective, such as current services estimates, and economic and accounting analyses.

- **Historical Tables**—provide data on budget receipts, outlays, surpluses or deficits, federal debt, and federal employment covering an extended time period.

Within a few days of the submission of the budget, the president also transmits an annual **Economic Report of the President** to Congress, which includes the report of the Council of Economic Advisors.

The president is required by law to update his submissions, and he does this in a far briefer, more summary fashion in his **Midsession Review**, which is due by July 15.

Online access to the president's budget documents is available in several places, including the Office of Management and Budget web site, *<www.whitehouse.gov/omb>*, and GPO Access, *<www.access.gpo.gov/usbudget>*.

From § 9.43, *Congressional Deskbook, <CongressionalDeskbook.com>*

Georgetown Law Library: Presidential Documents

<www.ll.georgetown.edu/guides/presidential_documents.cfm>

- This site provides information on print and online resources. Note that it is tailored for students using the Georgetown University Law Library.

State of the Union Addresses of the American Presidents
<www.asksam.com/ebooks/StateOfTheUnion/>

- Browse and search the full text of all State of the Union addresses from 1790 to present. This site is maintained by web software publisher askSam Systems.

§4.24 Office of Management and Budget Documents

The Office of Management and Budget (OMB) coordinates preparation of the president's budget, plays a leading role in its defense in Congress, and oversees implementation of the spending bills passed by Congress. OMB policies take many forms. The following types of publications contain instructions and guidelines to other federal entities from OMB:

- **Circulars**, expected to have a continuing effect of generally two years or more.

- **Bulletins**, containing guidance of a more transitory nature that would normally expire after one or two years.

- **Regulations** and **Paperwork**, daily reports that list regulations and paperwork under OMB review.

- **Financial Management** policies and **Grants Management** circulars and related documents.

- **Federal Register** submissions, including copies of proposed and final rules.

For information on OMB policies and publications, check the OMB web site *(<www.whitehouse.gov/omb>)* and the *Federal Register (at GPO Access, <www.gpoaccess.gov/fr/index.html>).*

From § 9.42, *Congressional Deskbook, <CongressionalDeskbook.com>*

§4.30 Agency Web Site Content

Federal department and agency web sites contain a wide array of information. Content varies from agency to agency, but federal agency web sites often include:

- Agency leadership biographies and speeches
- Annual reports and strategic plans
- Budget documents
- Congressional testimony from agency officials
- Databases and publications related to the regulatory, research, education, or outreach mission of the agency
- Educational materials for students and teachers
- Employee directories
- Freedom of Information Act (FOIA) instructions
- Inspector General reports
- Laws and regulations under which the agency operates or which they are responsible for enforcing
- Legal or administrative decisions, orders, or guidance issued by the agency
- News releases and media kits
- Organization charts
- Procurement, grants, or technology transfer opportunities

§4.40 Federal Regulations

For an overview of the federal regulatory process, see the Federal Regulatory Process Poster, by Ken Ackerman, ISBN 1-58733-013-X, TheCapitol.Net, 2006, *<RegulatoryProcess.com>*.

§4.41 Federal Register

Published by the Office of the Federal Register, National Archives and Records Administration (NARA), the *Federal Register* is the official daily publication for rules, proposed rules, and notices of federal agencies, as well as executive orders and other presidential documents.

Federal Register

<www.gpoaccess.gov/fr/>

Search or browse the full text of the *Federal Register*, from 1994 to present. Documents are available in HTML and PDF formats for 2000 to pres-

§4.42 Overview of the Rulemaking Process

1. Grant of rulemaking authority
- Congress delegates authority directly to agencies
- President may delegate constitutional authority to subordinates
- President or agency head may re-delegate authority to subordinates

2. Proposed Rule stage
- Office of Management and Budget (OMB) reviews under E.O. 12866
- Agencies publish Proposed Rule in *Federal Register* (FR) for public comment

3. Final Rule stage
- OMB reviews again under E.O. 12866
- Agencies publish final rule in FR
  - respond to comments, amend *Code of Federal Regulations*, set effective date

4. Congressional review
- Agencies submit rules to Congress and Government Accountability Office (could nullify rule)

5. Effective date
- Thirty-day minimum, sixty days for major rule, no minimum for good cause
- Agency may delay or withdraw rule before it becomes effective

ent, in plain text and PDF for 1995–2000, and in plain text only for 1994. The page also has a link to sign up to receive the daily *Federal Register* table of contents via email.

Federal Register—Documents on Public Inspection

<www.archives.gov/federal-register/public-inspection/>

A list of documents filed with the Office of the Federal Register that will be published in the *Register* in the immediate future.

Federal Register Tutorial

<www.archives.gov/federal-register/tutorial/index.html>

This tutorial can be viewed online in HTML or PDF format, or downloaded in its entirety. It explains the regulatory process, the *Federal Register*, and the *Code of Federal Regulations*. The tutorial page also links to guides on drafting documents for publication in the *Federal Register*.

§4.43 GPO Access: Federal Register

<www.gpoaccess.gov/fr/>

Scope:

- Issues of the *Federal Register* published from 1994 to the current issue.
- Links to page to sign up for daily *Federal Register* table of contents delivered via email.

Sponsor:

Government Printing Office. (Content is provided by the Office of the Federal Register, National Archives and Records Administration.)

Description:

The *Federal Register* is the official daily publication for rules, proposed rules, and notices of federal agencies and organizations, as well as executive orders and other presidential documents. GPO Access allows searches of the *Federal Register* by word for 1994 to present, and provides advanced searching and retrieval by page number for 1995 to present. The *Federal Register* is in text format for 1994, text and PDF for 1995–1999, and HTML and PDF for 2000 to present. Searchers can select a single year or search across a selection of years. Individual issues from 1998 to present can be browsed in HTML format.

Items in the *Federal Register* are cited by volume and page number, with year; for example:

69 Fed. Reg. 29171 (2004)

Search Tips:

Use "quotes" to find phrases.

Examples: "colorado river" "radiation exposure compensation act"

Search for agency names in quotes.

Examples: "fish and wildlife service" "national institutes of health"

Search for citations to affected sections of the *Code of Federal Regulations* in quotes:

Examples: "50 CFR Part 17" "28 CFR Part 79"

Use AND to combine two or more aspects of a complex search.

Examples: fisheries AND halibut

"fish and wildlife service" AND "sea turtle"

Use Advanced Search to limit searches to:
- A specific date or date range
- A specific section of the *Federal Register*, for example:
  - Final rules and regulations
  - Proposed rules and regulations
  - Notices (includes announcements of grant applications and public meetings)
  - Presidential documents (includes executive orders and proclamations)

§4.44 Code of Federal Regulations

The *Code of Federal Regulations* (CFR) is the codification of the general and permanent rules published in the *Federal Register* by the executive departments and agencies of the federal government. It is divided into fifty titles that represent broad areas subject to federal regulation. Each volume of the CFR is updated once each calendar year.

Code of Federal Regulations

<www.gpoaccess.gov/cfr/>

Search the CFR by word, retrieve CFR sections by citation, or browse by CFR title and part. Documents are in PDF and plain text formats. Editions of CFR titles are online for 1997 through the present; some 1996 titles are also available.

e-CFR

<www.gpoaccess.gov/ecfr/>

The CFR updated regularly with the new regulations that are issued throughout the year.

List of CFR Sections Affected

<*www.gpoaccess.gov/lsa/*>

The *List of CFR Sections Affected* (LSA) lists proposed, new, and amended federal regulations published in the *Federal Register* since the most recent revision date of a CFR title.

§4.45 GPO Access: Code of Federal Regulations

<*www.gpoaccess.gov/cfr/*>

Scope:

- Current text of the *Code of Federal Regulations* (*CFR*).
- Text of previous editions of the *CFR*, going back to 1996 or 1997, depending on title.

Sponsor:

Government Printing Office. (Content is provided by the Office of the Federal Register, National Archives and Records Administration.)

Description:

The CFR organizes the general and permanent regulations of executive branch departments and agencies into fifty broad subject areas, or titles, such as Energy, Internal Revenue, and Public Health. Each title is updated once each calendar year with the regulations issued in the *Federal Register* throughout the previous year: titles 1–16 are updated as of January 1; titles 17–27 as of April 1; titles 28–41 as of July 1; and titles 42–50 as of October 1.

Items in the CFR are typically cited by title and section, with year; for example:

34 C.F.R. § 1100.2 (2003)

GPO Access allows users to search the CFR by word, retrieve CFR sections by citation, or browse by CFR title and part.

Search Tips:

- Word searching works the same as in the *Federal Register* on GPO Access.
- To retrieve a known CFR citation, search for it in any of the following ways:
  - in the word search box in quotes, in this example format: "34CFR1100.2";

– with the Retrieve by CFR Citation fill-in search form; or

– with the Browse feature to select title, then part, then section.

- For a more precise search, use the Browse and/or Search feature and select a specific CFR title or titles to search within.

Updating the CFR:

CFR titles are only updated annually. A number of tools exist to help you learn if a CFR section has been changed by any new regulations since the CFR title was last updated. Options include:

- Searching the *Federal Register* for the time period since your CFR title was last updated
- Using the *List of Sections Affected* on GPO Access. Note: Although GPO Access includes instructions, this can be a tedious and confusing process.
- Using the GPO Access service called e-CFR (see page 64).

e-CFR

<www.gpoaccess.gov/ecfr/>

The e-CFR database is an electronic version of the CFR that is continuously updated as new regulations are issued. It can be browsed by title, part, and section, and has advanced search features.

§4.46 Code of Federal Regulations Titles

"The Code of Federal Regulations (CFR) is an annual codification of the general and permanent rules published in the *Federal Register* by the executive departments and agencies of the Federal Government.

"The CFR is divided into 50 titles representing broad areas subject to Federal regulation.

"Each Title is divided into chapters that are assigned to agencies issuing regulations pertaining to that broad subject area. Each chapter is divided into parts and each part is then divided into sections — the basic unit of the CFR.

"The purpose of the CFR is to present the official and complete text of agency regulations in one organized publication and to provide a comprehensive and convenient reference for all those who may need to know the text of general and permanent Federal regulations."

—The National Archives and Records Administration

<www.archives.gov/federal-register/cfr/about.html>

§4.47 CFR Titles

Title 1	General Provisions
Title 2	[Reserved]
Title 3	The President
Title 4	Accounts
Title 5	Administrative Personnel
Title 6	Homeland Security
Title 7	Agriculture
Title 8	Aliens and Nationality
Title 9	Animals and Animal Products
Title 10	Energy
Title 11	Federal Elections
Title 12	Banks and Banking
Title 13	Business Credit and Assistance
Title 14	Aeronautics and Space
Title 15	Commerce and Foreign Trade
Title 16	Commercial Practices
Title 17	Commodity and Securities Exchanges
Title 18	Conservation of Power and Water Resources
Title 19	Customs Duties
Title 20	Employees' Benefits
Title 21	Food and Drugs
Title 22	Foreign Relations
Title 23	Highways
Title 24	Housing and Urban Development
Title 25	Indians

(continued on page 66)

§4.47 CFR Titles (continued)

Title 26	Internal Revenue
Title 27	Alcohol, Tobacco Products, and Firearms
Title 28	Judicial Administration
Title 29	Labor
Title 30	Mineral Resources
Title 31	Money and Finance: Treasury
Title 32	National Defense
Title 33	Navigation and Navigable Waters
Title 34	Education
Title 35	Panama Canal
Title 36	Parks, Forests, and Public Property
Title 37	Patents, Trademarks, and Copyrights
Title 38	Pensions, Bonuses, and Veterans' Relief
Title 39	Postal Service
Title 40	Protection of Environment
Title 41	Public Contracts and Property Management
Title 42	Public Health
Title 43	Public Lands: Interior
Title 44	Emergency Management and Assistance
Title 45	Public Welfare
Title 46	Shipping
Title 47	Telecommunication
Title 48	Federal Acquisition Regulations System
Title 49	Transportation
Title 50	Wildlife and Fisheries

§4.48 Additional Regulatory Research Sources

Resources Covering All Agencies

OMB Office of Information and Regulatory Affairs (OIRA)—Regulatory Matters

<www.whitehouse.gov/omb/inforeg/regpol.html>

Includes lists of regulations currently under OMB review and those for which review has recently been completed; OMB prompt letters to agencies; and other resources.

Oversight Plans for All House Committees

<http://reform.house.gov>

Issued early in each Congress, this House report can be found on the House Government Reform Committee's web site, under the Reports section. It compiles House committee plans to review agency regulations, program implementation, and other matters.

Regulations.Gov

<www.regulations.gov>

Provides easy access to proposed regulations that are open for public comment and allows for submitting comments electronically.

The Unified Agenda

<www.gpoaccess.gov/ua/>

The Unified Agenda (also known as the Semiannual Regulatory Agenda) is published twice a year in the *Federal Register*. It summarizes the rules and proposed rules that each federal agency expects to issue during the next six months.

Agency Tools—Selected Examples

Small Business Administration Regulatory Alerts

<www.sba.gov/advo/laws/law_regalerts.html>

Lists documents published in the *Federal Register* and open for comment that may significantly affect small businesses. The alerts are issued by SBA's Office of Advocacy.

EPA—Federal Register Environmental Documents

<www.epa.gov/fedrgstr/>

Includes past EPA documents published in the *Federal Register* and an option to receive notices of new EPA *Federal Register* documents via email. Also features EPA's regulatory agenda.

USDA—Food Safety & Inspection Service (FSIS)—Regulations & Policies

<www.fsis.usda.gov/regulations_&_policies/index.asp>

Includes the regulatory agenda and FSIS documents published in the *Federal Register*.

Finding Aids and Guides

Georgetown University Law Library: Administrative Law Research

<www.ll.georgetown.edu/tutorials/admin/index.html>

Covers agency regulations and decisions. Written for GU law students, but of use to all.

RegInfo

<http://reginfo.gov>

Compilation of web links on federal regulations, maintained by the General Services Administration (GSA). Includes a colorful "Reg Map" that charts the regulatory process.

Regulatory Process Poster

<www.RegulatoryProcess.com>

A poster from TheCapitol.Net that outlines the federal regulatory process.

University of Virginia Library: Administrative Decisions & Other Actions

<www.lib.virginia.edu/govdocs/fed_decisions_agency.html>

Links to resources for administrative actions which are outside the scope of the *Code of Federal Regulations* or the *Federal Register*; for example, Revenue Rulings from the Internal Revenue Service and Directives from the Occupational Safety and Health Administration.

§4.50 Freedom of Information Act (FOIA)

The Freedom of Information Act (5 U.S.C. § 552) establishes the rules under which individuals can request and obtain access to unpublished records of federal executive branch agencies. Certain types of records—such as classified documents or those that would disclose confidential business information—are exempt from FOIA. In addition, FOIA does not apply to the federal judiciary or elected officials, including the president, vice president, and members of Congress. The requesting individual may have to pay a fee for the reproduction of the documents, and the processing time for FOIA requests can be lengthy.

Despite its limitations, many Washington researchers use FOIA as part of their information-gathering process. Some organizations routinely use FOIA to obtain documents and make them publicly available. As an example, see the National Security Archive at <*www.gwu.edu/~nsarchiv/*>.

§4.51 Resources for Learning About and Using FOIA

Most federal agencies have a link to FOIA information on their web sites.

"A Citizen's Guide on Using the Freedom of Information Act and the Privacy Act of 1974 to Request Government Records," House Report 108-172

<*http://reform.house.gov/UploadedFiles/FOIA%20Report.pdf*>

This guide is published each Congress by the House Government Reform Committee. The web address above is for the 108th Congress edition. For a current copy, see the reports section of the committee's web site, <*http://reform.house.gov*>.

Principal FOIA Contacts at Federal Agencies

<*www.justice.gov/04foia/foiacontacts.htm*>

This online directory from the Justice Department links to the FOIA web pages at federal agency web sites. It also provides name, address, and phone numbers for the agencies' FOIA contacts.

FOIA Reference Materials

<*www.usdoj.gov/04foia/04_7.html*>

The Justice Department links to a number of useful documents and guides on this page, including the *FOIA Post* newsletter and the text of the Freedom of Information Act.

Media Relations Handbook, by Brad Fitch
(TheCapitol.Net 2004)

<MediaRelationsHandbook.com>

Appendix 4, "Your Right to Federal Records: Questions and Answers on the Freedom of Information Act and Privacy Act."

§4.60 Federal Regulatory Agencies: Filings Databases

Federal regulations require certain individuals, companies, organizations, and other entities to file information with a government agency. This information is often available to the public via the Internet, although in some cases researchers must still go to public records rooms in Washington to retrieve documents.

The following list highlights some of the government filings databases available on the web:

FCC Radio and Television Station Filings
(page titled "CDBS Public Access")

<http://svartifoss2.fcc.gov/prod/cdbs/pubacc/prod/cdbs_pa.htm>

The Media Bureau of the Federal Communications Commission (FCC) regulates radio and television broadcasting. Their filings databases provide information on station ownership, mailing addresses, and other matters.

FEC Campaign Filings Reports and Data
(page titled "Campaign Finance Reports and Data")

<www.fec.gov/disclosure.shtml>

The Federal Election Commission (FEC) has financial filings from federal candidates, campaign committees, political parties, and political action committees. Several nongovernmental organizations make the same filings available online with additional search features or data compilations; a popular example is Opensecrets.org (*<www.opensecrets.org>*) from the Center for Responsive Politics.

SEC EDGAR
(page titled "SEC Filings & Forms (EDGAR)")

<www.sec.gov/edgar.shtml>

The Securities and Exchange Commission's EDGAR (Electronic Data Gathering, Analysis, and Retrieval) system makes public companies' SEC filings available online. SEC filings include information on finances, ownership, investors, executive compensation, and other matters. The SEC site provides a tutorial on using EDGAR. Several commercial online services provide fee-based access to the same filings, adding features such as better formatting of the corporate reports or more historical coverage.

Chapter 5

State and International Research

While this book focuses on national information resources, the Washington researcher often must consult state or international resources to track matters of interest. This section provides a brief introduction to some of the most helpful Internet resources for state and international research.

§5.00 State Government Information Resources

§5.01 Web Directories

National Governors Association's Governors Directory

<*www.nga.org/governors/*>

Includes brief biographies of each state or territorial governor.

State and Local Government on the Net

<*www.statelocalgov.net*>

Extensive directory of links to state and local government web sites. Also lists links to state offices by topic, such as attorneys general or public works departments.

State Court Web Sites

<*www.ncsconline.org/D_KIS/info_court_web_sites.html*>

Extensive list of links to state and local court web sites, from the National Center for State Courts.

State Election Officer Contact List

<*www.nass.org/electioninfo/state_contacts.htm*>

Phone numbers and web links for each state's elections director, from the National Association of Secretaries of State.

State Legislatures, State Laws, and State Regulations

<*www.llsdc.org/sourcebook/state-leg.htm*>

Web links and useful phone numbers for the state legislatures, with links to state laws and regulations online, from the Law Librarians' Society of Washington, DC.

WashLaw Web—StateLaw

<*www.washlaw.edu/uslaw/states/allstates/*>

Links to state governments, courts, and legislative and legal information, from Washburn University School of Law Library.

§5.02 Informational Sites

Census of Governments

<www.census.gov/govs/www/>

Data on state and local government finances, organization, and employment. Conducted and published every five years by the Census Bureau.

Georgetown University Law Center: State Laws

<www.ll.georgetown.edu/states/>

Web guides for doing legal research in each state or territory.

Stateline.org

<www.stateline.org>

News and profiles on issues of concern to state governments.

§5.10 International Research: Starting Points

§5.11 Search Engines and News

European Search Engines, Directories, and News

<www.netmasters.co.uk/european_search_engines/>

World Newspapers

<www.world-newspapers.com>

Yahoo! International Search Engines

<http://world.yahoo.com>

Country-specific versions of Yahoo! for selected countries in the Americas, Europe, Asia, and the Pacific. It also links to Spanish, Russian, and Chinese versions of the U.S. Yahoo!

§5.12 Business Information

Export.Gov Market Research

<www.export.gov/marketresearch.html>

Research reports on foreign markets. Free, but requires registration.

Global EDGE

<http://globaledge.MSU.edu>

Portal to international business information. Sponsored by Michigan State University.

World Pages

<http://global.wpz.com>

Links to online business and residential phone directories from around the world.

§5.13 Country Information

CIA—Chiefs of State and Cabinet Members of Foreign Governments

<www.cia.gov/cia/publications/chiefs/>

Continuously updated.

CIA—World Handbook

<www.cia.gov/cia/publications/factbook/>

Country profiles include map, national flag, and key facts on geography, demographics, government, economy, communications and transportation systems, and the military.

Library of Congress—Portals to the World

<www.loc.gov/rr/international/portals.html>

For each country, provides annotated list of links to web sites of research value, organized under topics such as Education, Health, Media, Religion, and Government/Politics.

State Department—Countries and Regions

<www.state.gov/travelandbusiness/>

Resources available here include: official list of country names; *Background Notes* on countries; and *The Diplomatic List* of diplomats at all foreign missions in the U.S.

§5.14 Laws and Treaties

ASIL (The American Society of International Law) Electronic Resource Guide to Treaties

<www.asil.org/resource/treaty1.htm>

Thorough guide to treaty research resources.

EISIL (Electronic Information System for International Law)

<www.eisil.org>

Links to online "primary materials, authoritative web sites, and helpful research guides to international law," organized under topics such as Use of Force and International Environmental Law.

JURIST—World Law

<http://jurist.law.pitt.edu/worldlaw/>

Describes and links to web sites on foreign countries' constitutional and legal systems. From the University of Pittsburgh School of Law.

Treaties in Force

<www.state.gov/s/l/treaties>

State Department publication listing treaties and other international agreements of the United States.

§5.20 International Organizations on the Web

§5.21 Finding Aids

Duke University Library: Non-Governmental Organizations Research Guide

<http://docs.lib.duke.edu/igo/guides/ngo/>

Links to international nongovernmental organizations (NGOs) organized alphabetically, geographically, by issue, and by affiliated international organizations (IGOs).

Northwestern University Library: Foreign Governments

<www.library.northwestern.edu/govpub/resource/internat/foreign.html>

List of links to the web sites for national governments, parliaments, central banks, and key ministries for foreign governments.

University of Michigan Library: International Agencies on the Web

<www.lib.umich.edu/govdocs/intl.html>

Extensive list of links to international agencies and groups such as the Asian Development Bank, the G-8 Summit, International Narcotics Board, and North Atlantic Treaty Organization (NATO). Also links to web sites on treaties and related issues.

§5.22 Selected International Governmental Organizations

European Union (EU)

<http://europa.eu.int/index_en.htm>

International Monetary Fund (IMF)

<www.imf.org>

United Nations

<www.un.org>

- InfoNation, *<www.cyberschoolbus.un.org/infonation/index.asp>* Find and compare national statistical data.

- Official Documents, *<http://documents.un.org>* Official United Nations documentation, from 1993 forward.

- United Nations Documentation: Research Guide, *<www.un.org/Depts/dhl/resguide/>* Guide to finding and understanding UN documents such as Security Council resolutions and voting records, both in print and online.

- United Nations News Service, *<www.un.org/News/>* Current news, statements, briefings.

- United Nations System of Organization, *<www.unsystem.org>* Web links to UN agencies, funds, and programs online. Linked agencies include Food and Agricultural Organization (FAO), International Atomic Energy Agency (IAEA), United Nations Educational, Scientific and Cultural Organization (UNESCO), United Nations High Commissioner for Refugees, World Health Organization (WHO), and many more.

World Bank Group

<www.worldbank.org>

World Intellectual Property Organization (WIPO)

<www.wipo.int>

World Trade Organization (WTO)

<www.wto.org>

Chapter 6

Experts and Insiders

Research Skills Series

Often the best research resource is a person, rather than a web site, database, or book. This section includes basic information on finding experts and obtaining information via phone calls.

§6.00 Offline Resources: People

Not all information is online, and much of it is not recorded anywhere but in the minds of experienced and knowledgeable people. Experts and insiders can be very helpful resources.

Your choice of phone or email may depend on how the source wishes to communicate. Email is convenient for people in other time zones, but can be limiting when you need to have an interactive conversation. Your interviews may also involve in-person meetings.

§6.01 When to Use People as an Information Source

✔ For information that has not been published online or in print.

✔ For opinions and insight into past, present, and future developments.

✔ For evaluative judgments about the information you have.

✔ For referrals to additional or better information sources.

✔ For a better understanding of how information and events are viewed by others.

§6.02 Preparing to Make an Information-Gathering Phone Call

✔ Make sure the answer is not readily available elsewhere.

✔ Do your homework. Try to get up to conversational level on a topic if you are calling an expert.

✔ Get background information on the person or organization you are calling to: a) confirm that this is an appropriate source and b) understand your source's role.

✔ Write down the questions you have or the information you need. Think about the best order in which to bring them up. While your conversation may not be a straight reading of questions, a list helps to ensure that you don't forget anything.

§6.03 Making the Call

✔ Introduce yourself by name and affiliation.

✔ Explain, concisely, why you are calling and how the information will be used ("I am writing a report for our membership and your work in this area is particularly important to us."). Let them know

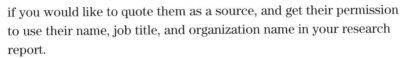

if you would like to quote them as a source, and get their permission to use their name, job title, and organization name in your research report.

✔ Listen to the response to be sure you have the proper person and that this is a good time to call.

✔ Ask your question, and then listen. Questions may be narrow ("Is this the correct title of the report?") or open-ended ("What do you think could happen next?").

✔ Don't worry when the conversation veers slightly off-topic. You may hear about facts or issues you had overlooked. At the very least, you will get a better understanding of what matters to your source.

✔ Don't hesitate to say that you are not sure you understand an issue. If necessary, restate what you think you understand and ask your contact if you have got it right.

✔ Wrap it up: Did you get all of the information you needed? Does the source have other sources to recommend? If necessary, can you make a follow-up call? What is the best time to call? Verify that you each have the other's phone number.

✔ Thank your contact, even if he or she has not been able to be helpful. If the source is important, you may wish to send a thank-you email or that rare species, the paper thank-you letter.

§6.10 Washington Contacts: Phone and Email

§6.11 Congress

Congressional staff can be useful sources of information on current congressional activities when that information is not available online, in print, or from other sources. Staff may be able to help you with future scheduling information or with very specific information on a bill they are currently handling.

Unfortunately, congressional staff phone directories are not available for free online. The Government Printing Office sells printed House and Senate telephone directories; see <*http://bookstore.gpo.gov*>. The Clerk of the House web site (<*http://clerk.house.gov*>) has House member and committee telephone directories, with links to Senate directories. However, the directories at the Clerk's site only provide the main office numbers; they do not list individual staff.

Several commercially published staff directories exist. For example, see the *Congressional Staff Directory* from Congressional Quarterly (*<http://csd.cq.com>*), the *Congressional Yellow Book* from Leadership Directories (*<www.leadershipdirectories.com/products/cyb.htm>*), or the *Congressional Directory* (*<www.CongressionalDirectory.com>*) from TheCapitol.Net.

Congressional staff members are usually very busy; do your research first and use them only as a last resort.

§6.12 Executive Departments and Agencies

Staff members at federal agencies include experts in an incredible range of specialties in science, agriculture, industry, trade, demographics, and many other fields. Agencies also include program staff members who can assist you with grants, economic development, research sponsorship, and other opportunities.

The Federal Citizen Information Center, maintained by the U.S. General Services Administration, has a page of links to federal employee phone directories, by agency; see *<www.info.gov/phone.htm>*. Some online agency directories include email addresses.

Commercially published directories of federal staff include Leadership Directories' *Federal Yellow Book* (*<www.leadershipdirectories.com/products/fyb.htm>*) and Carroll Publishing's *Federal Directory* (*<www.carrollpub.com/fedprint.asp>*), which also has federal legislative and judicial branch listings.

§6.13 Media Contacts

Reporters for trade journals and those who cover a specific topic may be willing to share information, particularly if you have information to share with them. If you are working in a particular issue area, it is beneficial to know the names of the media covering that topic in Washington.

Hudson's Washington News Media Contacts Directory (*<www.hudsonsdirectory.com>*) lists news services and syndicates, specialized newsletters, radio and TV stations, columnists, freelance writers, and the reporters representing U.S. national and local papers and foreign news services in Washington. The *News Media Yellow Book* (*<www.leadershipdirectories.com/products/nmyb.htm>*) includes media contact information nationwide as well as many foreign media contacts.

§6.14 Selected Media Web Sites

This is a selective list from the *Congressional Deskbook*, § 13.51, and is on the web as a sample section from the *Deskbook* at *<CongressionalDeskbook.com>*.

Print Newspapers Online

- Washington Post, *<www.washingtonpost.com>*
- Washington Times, *<www.washtimes.com>*
- Christian Science Monitor, *<www.christianscience monitor.com>*
- Los Angeles Times, *<www.latimes.com>*
- New York Times, *<www.nytimes.com>*
- Wall Street Journal, *<www.wsj.com>*

Hill Newspapers

- Roll Call, *<www.rollcall.com>*
- The Hill, *<www.thehill.com>*

Legal Affairs

- Legal Times, *<www.legaltimes.com>*
- National Law Journal, *<www.nlj.com>*

Television

- ABC News, *<http://abcnews.go.com>*
- BBC News, *<http://news.bbc.co.uk>*
- C-SPAN, *<www.c-span.org>*
- CBS News, *<www.cbsnews.com>*
- CNN, *<www.cnn.com>*
- FOX News, *<www.foxnews.com>*
- NBC News, *<www.nbc.com/nbc/NBC_News/>*
- NewsHour with Jim Lehrer, *<www.pbs.org/newshour/>*

Radio

- C-SPAN Radio, *<www.c-span.org>*
- FederalNewsRadio.com, *<http://federalnewsradio.com>*
- National Public Radio, *<www.npr.org>*
- WTOP, *<www.wtopnews.com>*

On the Wires

- Associated Press, *<www.ap.org>*
- Reuters, *<www.reuters.com>*
- US Newswire, *<www.usnewswire.com/topnews/current.htm>*
- Voice of America News, *<www.voanews.com>*

Weekly Magazines

- CQ Weekly, *<www.cq.com>*
- Economist, *<www.economist.com>*
- National Journal, *<http://nationaljournal.com>*
- Newsweek, *<www.newsweek.com>*
- Time, *<www.time.com/time/>*
- US News and World Report, *<www.usnews.com/usnews/home.htm>*

Other

- National Press Club, *<http://npc.press.org>*

§6.15 **Think Tanks**

Washington think tanks or policy research institutes typically have an online directory of their subject experts, including email addresses, on their web sites. (For more information, see § 6.20, Think Tanks Online.)

§6.16 **Trade and Professional Associations**

Numerous national and international trade associations represent their members' interests in Washington. The larger associations have experts on industry and trade issues on staff. They can be a helpful source for legislative, regulatory, and other information specific to the association's concerns. The smaller associations may also be able to provide you with the information you need, or they may refer you to a contact elsewhere.

Among the larger industry associations that cover a wide range of issues are the United States Chamber of Commerce, *<www.uschamber.com>*; National Association of Manufacturers, *<www.nam.org>*; and National Federation of Independent Businesses, *<www.nfib.com>*. Major professional associations include the American Medical Association, *<www.ama-assn.org>*, and the National Education Association, *<www.nea.org>*. The Independent Sector, *<www.independentsector.org>*, represents nonprofit and philanthropic organizations.

Trade and professional association web sites usually do not include contact information for individual staff. Aside from a main number, they often provide email forms for submitting any inquiries not answered by the content on their web site.

Commercially published directories for associations include Leadership Directories' *Association Yellow Book* (*<www.leadershipdirectories.com/products/ayb.htm>*) and the *National Trade and Professional Associations of the United States* from Columbia Books (*<www.associationexecs.com>*).

The American Society of Association Executives provides a searchable database, called *Gateway to Associations*, on its web site (*<www.asaenet.org>*). To get there, choose "Directories" from the main menu, then choose "Associations" and select "Gateway to Associations."

§6.20 **Think Tanks Online**

"Think tank" is the popular name for a variety of organizations that conduct public policy research and education. Typically, they are nonprofit organizations. They may be independent or affiliated with a university, foundation, or other institution. They maintain staffs of specialized policy experts; they may also host visiting experts or contract with outside experts for research. Some cover a wide range of public policy issues, while others focus on a topic such as education, defense, or the federal budget. Many are associated with a specific ideology, such as limited government or the promotion of human rights.

Think-tank experts write reports and journal articles, give speeches and policy briefings, sit on discussion panels, and lead educational programs. Much of their work can be found on the think tanks' web sites.

Resources commonly found on think-tank web sites include:

- Directories of their experts or staff subject expertise, with the experts' email addresses (sometimes found in the About Us section).
- A news/press/media center highlighting recent publications and statements on topical issues.
- Links to the text of their reports, briefings, and other releases organized by topic.
- An events section listing upcoming briefings and policy forums (often with the archived audio, video, or printed transcript for past events).
- An online book store, with policy books for purchase.

§6.21 Finding Think Tanks Online

The following sites provide links to many U.S. think-tank web sites:

Think Tanks and Public Interest Organizations

<http://usinfo.state.gov/usa/infousa/politics/thnktank.htm>

A selective list of links, from the State Department's infoUSA web site for foreign audiences seeking information on U.S. politics and policy.

Yahoo! Directory: Public Policy> Institutes

*<http://dir.yahoo.com/Social_Science/
political_science/public_policy/institutes/>*

A more extensive list of links, with brief descriptions.

In addition, the National Journal Inc. publishes a Washington directory called *The Capital Source* that includes a listing of Washington think tanks. Other sections in *The Capital Source* list contact information for Congress, the White House, the news media, trade associations, law and lobbying firms, and interest groups. For more information, see *<http://nationaljournal.com/about/capitalsource/>*.

§6.22 Selected Policy Institutes and Think Tanks

This is a selective list from the *Congressional Deskbook*, § 13.52, and is on the web as a sample section from the *Deskbook* at *<CongressionalDeskbook.com>*.

- American Enterprise Institute for Public Policy Research, *<www.aei.org>*
- Brookings Institution, *<www.brookings.org>*
- Carl Albert Congressional Research & Studies Center, *<www.ou.edu/special/albertctr/cachome.html>*
- Carnegie Endowment for International Peace, *<www.carnegieendowment.org>*
- Cato Institute, *<www.cato.org>*
- Center for American Progress, *<www.americanprogress.org>*
- Center for Congressional and Presidential Studies, *<http://spa.american.edu/ccps/>*
- Center for National Policy, *<www.cnponline.org>*
- Center for Strategic and International Studies, *<www.csis.org>*
- Center on Congress, <http://*congress.indiana.edu*>
- Center on Budget and Policy Priorities, *<www.cbpp.org>*
- Council on Foreign Relations, *<www.cfr.org>*
- Dirksen Congressional Center, *<www.dirksencongressionalcenter.org>*
- Heritage Foundation, *<www.heritage.org>*
- James A. Baker III Institute for Public Policy, *<http://bakerinstitute.org>*
- Joint Center for Political and Economic Studies, *<www.jointcenter.org>*
- National Bureau for Economic Research, *<www.nber.org>*
- National Center for Policy Analysis, *<www.ncpa.org>*
- Progressive Policy Institute, *<www.ppionline.org>*
- The Public Forum Institute, *<www.publicforuminstitute.org>*
- Urban Institute, *<www.urban.org>*
- Woodrow Wilson International Center for Scholars, *<www.wilsoncenter.org>*

Table of Web Sites

Name	URL	Section
ABC News	http://abcnews.go.com	6.14
Administrative Office of the U.S. Courts	www.uscourts.gov	3.30
American Enterprise Institute for Public Policy Research	www.aei.org	6.22
American Medical Association	www.ama-assn.org	6.16
American Presidency Project	www.presidency.ucsb.edu	4.22
Appropriations, FY 2006	http://thomas.loc.gov/home/approp/app06.html	2.40
ASAE Gateway to Associations	www.asaenet.org	6.16
ASIL (The American Society of International Law) Electronic Resource Guide to Treaties	www.asil.org/resource/treaty1.htm	5.14
Ask.com	www.ask.com	1.01
Associated Press	www.ap.org	6.14
Association Yellow Book	www.leadershipdirectories.com/products/ayb.htm	6.16
BBC News	http://news.bbc.co.uk	6.14
beSpacific	www.bespacific.com	1.53
Bloglines.com	www.bloglines.com	1.54
Brookings Institution	www.brookings.org	6.22
Capital Source, The	http://nationaljournal.com/about/capitalsource	6.21
Carl Albert Congressional Research & Studies Center	www.ou.edu/special/albertctr/cachome.html	6.22
Carnegie Endowment for International Peace	www.carnegieendowment.org	6.22
Cato Institute	www.cato.org	6.22
CBS News	www.cbsnews.com	6.14
Census of Governments	www.census.gov/govs/www	5.02

Name	URL	Section
Center for American Progress	**www.americanprogress.org**	6.22
Center for Congressional and Presidential Studies	**http://spa.american. edu/ccps**	6.22
Center for National Policy	**www.cnponline.org**	6.22
Center for Strategic and International Studies	**www.csis.org**	6.22
Center on Congress	**http://congress. indiana.edu**	6.22
Center on Budget and Policy Priorities	**www.cbpp.org**	6.22
Christian Science Monitor	**www.christianscience monitor.com**	6.14
CIA	**www.cia.gov/cia/ publications/chiefs**	5.13
	www.cia.gov/cia/ publications/factbook	5.13
Clerk of the House	**http://clerk.house.gov/hist High/Congressional_History/ Session_Dates/index.html**	2.14
	http://clerk.house.gov	6.11
CNN	**www.cnn.com**	6.14
Code of Federal Regulations	**www.gpoaccess.gov/cfr**	4.44; 4.45
	www.archives.gov/federal- register/cfr/about.html	4.46
Congressional Bills: Glossary	**www.gpoaccess.gov/ bills/glossary.html**	2.15
Congressional Budget Office	**www.cbo.gov/pubs_ index.cfm**	2.50
Congressional Staff Directory	**http://csd.cq.com**	6.11
Congressional Yellow Book	**www.leadershipdirectories. com/products/cyb.htm**	6.11
Consumer Product Safety Commission	**www.cpsc.gov/cpscpub/ prerel/prerel.html**	1.55
Congressional Research Service	**www.loc.gov/crsinfo**	2.81
Council on Foreign Relations	**www.cfr.org**	6.22

Name	URL	Section
CQ.com	**www.cq.com**	1.56; 2.50
CQ Weekly	**www.cq.com**	6.14
CRS Reports	**www.llrx.com/features/ crsreports.htm**	2.81
C-SPAN	**www.c-span.org**	6.14
C-SPAN Radio	**www.c-span.org**	6.14
Dirksen Congressional Center	**www.dirksen congressionalcenter.org**	6.22
DocuTicker	**www.docuticker.com**	1.53
Dogpile	**www.dogpile.com**	1.01
Duke Univ. Library	**http://docs.lib.duke. edu/igo/guides/ngo**	5.21
e-CFR	**www.gpoaccess.gov/ecfr**	4.44; 4.45
Economist	**www.economist.com**	6.14
Electronic Information System for International Law	**www.eisil.org**	5.14
EPA—Federal Register Environmental Documents	**www.epa.gov/fedrgstr**	4.48
European Search Engines, Directories, and News	**www.netmasters.co.uk/ european_search_engines**	5.11
Executive Order disposition tables	**www.archives.gov/federal- register/executive-orders/ disposition.html**	4.21
European Union	**http://europa.eu.int/ index_en.htm**	5.22
Export.Gov Market Research	**www.export.gov/ marketresearch.html**	5.12
FactCheck.org	**www.factcheck.org**	1.42
FCC Radio and Television Station Filings	**http://svartifoss2.fcc.gov/ prod/cdbs/pubacc/prod/ cdbs_pa.htm**	4.60
FEC Campaign Filings Reports	**www.fec.gov/ disclosure.shtml**	4.60
Federal Citizen Information Center	**www.info.gov/phone.htm**	6.12

Name	URL	Section
Federal Directory	**www.carrollpub.com/ fedprint.asp**	6.12
Federal Judicial Opinions	**www.law.cornell.edu/ federal/opinions.html**	3.30
Federal Judicial Vacancies	**www.uscourts.gov/ judicialvac.html**	3.30
FederalNewsRadio.com	**http://federal newsradio.com**	6.14
Federal Legislative History Documents	**www.llsdc.org/sourcebook/ docs/elec-leg-hist-docs.pdf**	2.20
Federal Register	**www.gpoaccess.gov/fr/**	1.37; 4.24; 4.41; 4.43
	http://listserv. access.gpo.gov	1.51
	www.archives.gov/federal-register/public-inspection	4.41
	www.archives.gov/federal-register/tutorial/index.html	4.41
Federal Yellow Book	**www.leadershipdirectories. com/products/fyb.htm**	6.12
FindLaw	**www.findlaw.com**	1.11; 3.20
	http://dictionary.lp. findlaw.com	3.50
FirstGov	**www.firstgov.gov**	Ch. 4; 4.10
	www.firstgov.gov/Topics/ Reference_Shelf/Libraries/ RSS_Library.shtml	1.55
Fox News	**www.foxnews.com**	6.14
Freedom of Information Act	**http://reform.house.gov/ UploadedFiles/FOIA%20 Report.pdf**	4.51
	www.justice.gov/04foia/ foiacontacts.htm	4.51
	www.usdoj.gov/04foia/ 04_7.html	4.51
GalleryWatch	**www.gallerywatch.com**	1.56; 2.50

Name	URL	Section
Georgetown Univ.	**www.ll.georgetown.edu/ find/**	1.11; 3.30
	www.ll.georgetown.edu/ guides/presidential_ documents.cfm	4.22
	www.ll.georgetown.edu/ tutorials/admin/index.html	4.48
	www.ll.georgetown.edu/ states/	5.02
Global EDGE	**http://globaledge.MSU.edu**	5.12
Google	**www.google.com**	1.01
	www.google.com/unclesam	1.20
	www.google.com/ help/index.html	1.32
Government Accountability Office	**www.gao.gov/subtest/ subscribe.html**	2.50
Government Printing Office	**www.gpoaccess.gov**	2.70; 6.11
GPO Access	**www.gpoaccess.gov**	1.30; 1.37; Ch. 2; 2.20; 2.60; 4.00; 4.21; 4.23; 4.24; 4.41; 4.43; 4.44; 4.45; 4.48
GPO Federal Depository Library Directory	**www.gpoaccess.gov/ libraries.html**	2.60
GPO Online Bookstore	**http://bookstore.gpo.gov**	2.60
Heritage Foundation	**www.heritage.org**	6.22
Hill, The	**www.thehill.com**	6.14
House Appropriations Committee	**http://appropriations. house.gov**	2.41
House Majority Whip	**http://majoritywhip. house.gov/Resources.asp**	1.51; 2.50
House Minority Whip	**http://democraticwhip. house.gov**	1.51
	http://democraticwhip. house.gov/whip/daily.cfm	2.50

Name	URL	Section
Hudson's Washington News Media Contacts Directory	**www.hudsonsdirectory.com**	6.13
Independent Sector, The	**www.independent sector.org**	6.16
InfoPeople	**http://infopeople.org/ search/guide.html**	1.03
	http://infopeople.org/ search/chart.html	1.03
International Monetary Fund (IMF)	**www.imf.org**	5.22
Internet Public Library	**www.ipl.org**	1.11
James A. Baker III Institute for Public Policy	**http://bakerinstitute.org**	6.22
Joint Center for Political and Economic Studies	**www.jointcenter.org**	6.22
Judges of the United States Courts	**www.fjc.gov/history/ home.nsf**	3.30
JURIST—World Law	**http://jurist.law.pitt. edu/worldlaw**	5.14
Legal Information Institute	**www.law.cornell.edu**	2.60; 2.70; 3.20; 3.30; 3.40; 4.10
Legal Times	**www.legaltimes.com**	6.14
LexisNexis	**www.lexisnexis.com**	1.56; 2.50; Ch. 3
Librarian's Index to the Internet	**http://lii.org**	1.11
Library of Congress	**www.loc.gov/rr/ international/portals.html**	5.13
List of CFR Sections Affected	**www.gpoaccess.gov/lsa**	4.44
Lobbyist Registrations	**http://sopr.senate.gov**	2.82
Los Angeles Times	**www.latimes.com**	6.14
Media Relations Handbook	**www.MediaRelations Handbook.com**	4.51
MSN Search	**http://search.msn.com**	1.01
National Archives	**www.archives.gov**	1.61; 2.60; 4.21; 4.41

Name	URL	Section
National Association of Manufacturers	**www.nam.org**	6.16
National Bureau for Economic Research	**www.nber.org**	6.22
National Center for Policy Analysis	**www.ncpa.org**	6.22
National Education Association	**www.nea.org**	6.16
National Federation of Independent Businesses	**www.nfib.com**	6.16
National Governors Association's Governors Directory	**www.nga.org/governors**	5.01
National Journal	**http://nationaljournal.com**	6.14
National Law Journal	**www.nlj.com**	6.14
National Press Club	**http://npc.press.org**	6.14
National Public Radio	**www.npr.org**	6.14
National Security Archive	**www.gwu.edu/~nsarchiv**	4.50
National Trade and Professional Associations of the United States	**www.associationexecs.com**	6.16
NBC News	**www.nbc.com/nbc/NBC_News**	6.14
NewsHour with Jim Lehrer	**www.pbs.org/newshour**	6.14
News Media Yellow Book	**www.leadershipdirectories.com/products/nmyb.htm**	6.13
Newsweek	**www.newsweek.com**	6.14
New York Times	**www.nytimes.com**	6.14
Northwestern Univ. Library: Foreign Governments	**www.library.northwestern.edu/govpub/resource/internat/foreign.html**	5.21
Office of Management and Budget	**www.whitehouse.gov/omb**	4.23; 4.24
	www.whitehouse.gov/omb/inforeg/regpol.html	4.48
OpenCRS	**www.opencrs.com**	2.81
Oversight Plans for House Committees	**http://reform.house.gov**	4.48

Name	URL	Section
President's Budget Documents		
GPO Access	**www.access.gpo.gov/ usbudget**	4.23
Office of Management and Budget	**www.whitehouse.gov/omb**	4.23
Presidential Documents	**www.archives.gov/ presidential-libraries/ research/guide.html**	4.21
Presidential Libraries	**www.archives.gov/ presidential-libraries**	4.21
Progressive Policy Institute	**www.ppionline.org**	6.22
Public Agenda	**www.publicagenda.org/ issues/issuehome.cfm**	1.11
	www.publicagenda.org	1.42
Public Forum Institute, The	**www.publicforum institute.org**	6.22
Public Laws Electronic Notification Service	**www.archives.gov/federal register/laws/updates.html**	1.51
RegInfo	**http://reginfo.gov**	4.48
Regulations.Gov	**www.regulations.gov**	4.48
ResearchBuzz	**www.researchbuzz.com**	1.38
Reuters	**www.reuters.com**	6.14
Roll Call	**www.rollcall.com**	6.14
SCOTUSblog	**www.scotusblog.com**	1.53
Search Engine Watch	**http://searchengine watch.com**	1.38
SEC EDGAR	**www.sec.gov/edgar.shtml**	4.60
Senate Appropriations Committee	**http://appropriations. senate.gov**	2.41
Senate Majority Whip	**http://mcconnell.senate. gov/whip_office.cfm**	1.51; 2.50
Small Business Administration Regulatory Alerts	**www.sba.gov/advo/ laws/law_regalerts.html**	4.48
Snopes.com Urban Legend	**www.snopes.com**	1.42
Soople	**www.soople.com**	1.01
State and Local Governments	**www.statelocalgov.net**	5.01

Name	URL	Section
State Courts	**www.ncsconline.org/D_KIS/ info_court_web_sites.html**	5.01
State Election Officer Contact List	**www.nass.org/electioninfo/ state_contacts.htm**	5.01
State Legislatures, State Laws, and State Regulations	**www.llsdc.org/ sourcebook/state-leg.htm**	5.01
Stateline.org	**www.stateline.org**	1.11; 5.02
State of the Union Addresses	**www.asksam.com/ebooks/ StateOfTheUnion**	4.22
Statutes at Large		
GPO Federal Depository Library Directory	**www.gpoaccess.gov/ libraries.html**	2.60
GPO Online Bookstore	**http://bookstore.gpo.gov**	2.60
Supreme Court Opinions		
FindLaw	**www.findlaw.com/ casecode/supreme.html**	3.20
	http://supreme.lp. findlaw.com/supreme_ court/resources.html	3.20
Legal Information Institute	**http://supct.law. cornell.edu/supct**	3.20
U.S. Supreme Court	**www.supremecourtus.gov**	3.20
TheCapitol.Net	**www.TheCapitol.Net**	2.00
Congressional and Legislative Terms	**www.thecapitol.net/ glossary**	2.15
Congressional Deskbook	**www.Congressional Deskbook.com**	2.00; 2.41; 2.43; 2.51; 4.23; 4.24; 6.14; 6.22
Congressional Directory	**www.Congressional Directory.com**	6.11
Congressional Documents	**www.congressional documents.com**	2.20
Federal Regulatory Process Poster	**www.Regulatory Process.com**	4.40; 4.48
Legal Reference and Research Tools	**www.thecapitol.net/ Research/legalFTL.htm**	Ch. 3

Name	URL	Section
Think Tanks and Public Interest Organizations	http://usinfo.state.gov/usa/infousa/politics/thnktank.htm	6.21
THOMAS	http://thomas.loc.gov	Ch. 2; 2.20; 2.30; 2.60
Time	www.time.com/time	6.14
Treaties in Force	www.state.gov/s/l/treaties	5.14
Unified Agenda, The	www.gpoaccess.gov/ua	4.48
United Nations	www.un.org	5.22
Urban Institute	www.urban.org	6.22
U.S. Chamber of Commerce	www.uschamber.com	6.16
U.S. Code		
GPO Access	www.gpoaccess.gov/uscode	2.60; 2.70
House Law Revision Counsel	http://uscode.house.gov	2.60
Legal Information Institute	www.law.cornell.edu/uscode	2.60; 2.70
LexisNexis	www.lexisnexis.com	2.60
Westlaw	http://west.thomson.com/store	2.60
U.S. Court of Federal Claims	www.uscfc.uscourts.gov	3.00
U.S. Court of International Trade	www.cit.uscourts.gov	3.00
U.S. Court of Veterans Appeals	www.vetapp.gov	3.00
U.S. Courts of Appeal	www.uscourts.gov/courtlinks/	3.00; 3.10
USDA		
Food Safety & Inspection Service	www.fsis.usda.gov/regulations_&_policies/index.asp	4.48
U.S. District Courts	www.uscourts.gov/courtlinks/	3.00
U.S. Government Internet Manual	www.bernanpress.com	1.12

Name	URL	Section
U.S. House of Representatives	**www.house.gov**	Ch. 2
US News and World Report	**www.usnews.com/ usnews/home.htm**	6.14
US Newswire	**www.usnewswire.com/ topnews/current.htm**	6.14
U.S. Senate	**www.senate.gov**	Ch. 2
U.S. State Department	**www.state.gov/ misc/52620.htm**	1.55
	www.state.gov/ travelandbusiness	5.13
U.S. Supreme Court	**www.supremecourtus.gov**	3.00; 3.20
U.S. Tax Court	**www.ustaxcourt.gov**	3.00
Univ. of Michigan	**www.lib.umich.edu/ govdocs/index.html**	1.11
	www.lib.umich.edu/ govdocs/intl.html	5.21
Univ. of Virginia Library	**www.lib.virginia.edu/ govdocs/fed_decisions_ agency.html**	3.00; 4.48
Virtual Chase, The	**www.virtualchase.com**	1.38
Voice of America News	**www.voanews.com**	6.14
Wall Street Journal	**www.wsj.com**	6.14
Washington Information Directory	**www.cqpress.com**	1.12
Washington Post	**www.washingtonpost.com**	6.14
Washington Times	**www.washtimes.com**	6.14
WashLaw Web	**www.washlaw.edu/ uslaw/states/allstates**	5.01
Westlaw	**http://west.thomson.com**	1.56; 2.50; 2.60; Ch. 3
White House	**www.whitehouse.gov**	4.21
Whois Source	**www.allwhois.com**	1.44
	www.whois.sc	1.44
World Bank Group	**www.worldbank.org**	5.22

Name	URL	Section
World Intellectual Property Organization	www.wipo.int	5.22
World Newspapers	www.world-newspapers.com	5.11
World Pages	http://global.wpz.com	5.12
World Trade Organization (WTO)	www.wto.org	5.22
Woodrow Wilson International Center for Scholars	www.wilsoncenter.org	6.22
WTOP	www.wtopnews.com	6.14
Yahoo!	http://search.yahoo.com	1.01
	http://help.yahoo.com/help/us/ysearch	1.32
	http://dailynews.yahoo.com	1.55
	http://news.yahoo.com/rss	1.55
	http://world.yahoo.com	5.11
	http://dir.yahoo.com/Social_Science/political_science/public_policy/institutes	6.21

Index

About Us

TheCapitol.Net is a non-partisan small business that provides continuing professional education and publications for thousands of government and business leaders each year. TheCapitol.Net came out of Congressional Quarterly, which had offered many of our training courses since the late 1970s. TheCapitol.Net is the exclusive provider of Congressional Quarterly (CQ) Executive Conferences.

Courses

We offer practical legislative, advocacy and media training in various educational tracks for all levels of federal agency, corporate and association staff, taught by our expert faculty, all of whom are independent, subject matter experts.

Our courses are approved for CEU credits from George Mason University.

Publications

We publish hands-on books for practitioners, written by subject matter experts, including: *Congressional Deskbook; Real World Research; Congressional Directory; Legislative Drafter's Deskbook; Congressional Operations Poster; Media Relations Handbook;* and *Common Sense Rules of Advocacy.*

Convenience Learning

If you don't have time to attend one of our live courses in Washington, DC, we offer other ways for you to learn how Washington works.™

Telephone Seminars

Our telephone seminars are an easy and economical way to learn from our expert faculty. Telephone seminars include a Q&A session so you have an opportunity to talk with the faculty. The registration fee covers as many as 10 people listening on a speaker phone.

Audio CDs

We offer our telephone seminars as audio CDs that you can listen to anytime—car, exercising, home, office, Metro or train, plane.

Custom, On-Site Training

All of our courses can be tailored for on-site training.

We design each custom training program to meet your educational and training goals, and then select faculty who can best meet those objectives and who are best suited for your attendees.

We have tailored hundreds of outstanding on-site training programs for agencies, law and lobbying firms, unions, foreign delegations, associations and corporations that show how Washington works.™

Our custom training courses can include CEU credits from George Mason University.

Faculty and Authors

We identify, recruit, and work with outstanding faculty and authors to bring their expertise to professional markets in spoken, written, and online formats.

Clients

Our 1,000-plus clients include all three branches of government and large and small organizations from across the country.

TheCapitol.Net

Non-partisan training and publications that show how Washington works.™

PO Box 25706, Alexandria, VA 22313-5706 202-678-1600 www.TheCapitol.Net

Exclusive provider of Congressional Quarterly Executive Conferences

Capitol Hill Workshop
Politics, Policy, and Process

Our Capitol Hill Workshop gives you an overview of the legislative
process while highlighting the forces that influence decision making
in Congress. You will leave the course with an understanding of:

- Congressional procedure and the legislative process.
- Politics and leadership in the Congress.
- Congressional budgeting today.
- The role of OMB in the legislative process.
- Influencing Washington—How to communicate effectively
  with Congress.
- How media covers the big beats.
- The current trends in campaigns and elections.
- How members of Congress advance their legislative and
  political agendas.
- The work of personal and committee staff and how you can
  build strong working relationships with staffers.

A wide range of current experts provide insight into every aspect
of Congress—how Capitol Hill interacts with the White House and
executive agencies, lobbyists, the media, interest groups, and more.
Attend a congressional hearing and see the process in action. You also
receive a wealth of course materials, including the *Congressional Deskbook*.

Offered several times each year in Washington, DC.

For more information,
call TheCapitol.Net at 202-678-1600, or see
www.CapitolHillWorkshop.com

How to Research and Compile Legislative Histories:
Searching for Legislative Intent

This full-day course is for you if your work requires that you locate, compile and analyze legislative histories of federal laws.

We demonstrate and discuss:

- The different types of documents (enacted laws, bills and resolutions, floor debates, committee reports and documents) needed to research and compile legislative histories will be explained (the focus will be federal, not state, legislative history research methodologies).

- The fastest ways to find and use these documents— in print and online.

- Our expert faculty share their secrets and tips.

Please note: the focus of this course is on federal law.

Offered several times each year in Washington, DC.

*For more information,
call TheCapitol.Net at 202-678-1600, or see*
www.LegislativeResearch.com